Welcome to the Huge History Quiz Book

Lunar Press is a privately-run publishing company which cares greatly about the accuracy of its content.

As many questions in this quiz book are subject to change, please email us at lunarpresspublishing@gmail.com if you notice any inaccuracies to help us keep our questions as up-to-date as possible.

Happy Quizzing!

CONTENTS

PRE-HISTORY

1. Place the Bronze, Stone and Iron Age in chronological order.

2. Roughly how many years ago did humans diverge from apes?
a. 200,000 years ago   b. 10 million years ago
c. 1.2 billion years ago   d. 120 million years ago

3. True or false: humans and dinosaurs coexisted.

4. How many major Ice Ages have there been on Earth?
a. 2   b. 3   c. 4   d. At least 5

5. In which era would you find the Tyrannosaurus Rex?
a. Jurassic   b. Triassic   c. Stone Age   d. Cretaceous

6. What marked the end of the pre-historic period?

7. The first instrument was found 60,000 years ago. What was it?
a. Drum   b. Flute   c. Guitar   d. Xylophone

8. Which species of early human are known as 'the hobbits'?
a. Homo floresiensis   b. Homo erectus
c. Homo habilis   d. Homo neanderthalensis

9. Which species of early human lived on Earth 9 times longer than our own species?
a. Homo floresiensis   b. Homo erectus
c. Homo habilis   d. Homo neanderthalensis

10. The word 'prehistory' comes from which language?
a. Latin   b. Tamil   c. Ancient Greek   d. Sanskrit

ANCIENT EGYPT

1. Which ancient artefact helped us to understand hieroglyphics?

2. Name the famous ruler who conquered Egypt in 332 BC.

3. What is the name of the book that helped ancient Egyptians prepare for the afterlife?

4. What was the name of the archaeologist who discovered Tutankhamun's tomb?

5. What was the main reason that the Egyptian civilization settled by the River Nile?
a. It provided rich and fertile soil for growing crops
b. For a reliable food source
c. It let them transport goods via boat
d. For a constant supply of drinking water

6. In which year was Tutankhamun's tomb found?
a. 1900   b. 1922   c. 1934   d. 1943

7. What type of people formed the upper class in ancient Egypt, known as the "white kilt class"?
a. The rich and wealthy   b. Priests and other religious officials
c. Scribes and officials   d. People related to Pharaohs

8. Ramses III was the pharaoh of which ancient Egyptian dynasty?
a. 18th Dynasty   b. 19th Dynasty   c. 20th Dynasty

9. Which goddess in Ancient Egypt mythology liked to drink blood?
a. Wadjet   b. Renenutet   c. Nephthys   d. Sekhmet

10. How many mummies were found in the Great Pyramid of Giza?
a. 0   b. 5   c. 10   d. 15

11. What is the name of the Ancient Egyptian God of the dead?
a. Osiris   b. Isis   c. Anubis   d. Horus

12. What was the first body part to be removed during the mummification process?
a. Brain   b. Heart   c. Liver   d. Kidney

13. Which mineral were the corpses left in for 70 days during the mummification process?

14. What was a body stuffed with during the mummification process, to give the body a more human shape?
a. Sand mixed with water   b. Soil   c. Sand and linen   d. Horses hair

15. What did the eye of Horus (or 'wedjat eye') symbolise?
a. Protection from evil   b. Courage to go to war
c. Foresight into the future   d. Prosperity for your family

16. Akhet (flooding) and Peret (planting) are two of the three seasons the Ancient Egyptians recognised, what is the name of the third season?

17. What years did the Old Kingdom period take place?
a. 2649–2130 BC   b. 2181-2055 BC   c. 1550-1069 BC   d. 2055-1650 BC

18. What was the name of the place where the Egyptians buried their kings in tombs?

19. Pharaohs often wore the symbol of a serpent on their crowns to serve as protectors of Lower Egypt. Which serpent was this?
a. Rattlesnake   b. Cobra   c. Python   d. Black Mamba

20. Nefertiti was the wife of which Pharaoh?
a. Khufu   b. Djoser   c. Akhenaten   d. Ramses II

21. Scientists have recently found DNA in King Tutankhamun's tomb confirming multiple strains of which infection?
a. Tuberculosis   b. Cholera   c. Typhoid   d. Malaria

22. Which two powerful Roman Generals is Cleopatra VII said to have had romantic relationships with?
a. Julius Caesar   b. Gaius Marius   c. Scipio Africanus   d. Mark Antony

23. What year did Egypt become part of the Roman Empire which subsequently ended the age of the Pharaohs?
a. 280 BC   b. 120 BC   c. 30 BC   d. 110 AD

24. Cleopatra VII is said to have killed herself by encouraging what poisonous animal to bite her?

25. How old was Tutankhamun thought to be when he died?
a. 15   b. 19   c. 24   d. 30

26. How many years was Tutankhamun's tomb left undisturbed?
a. 1000 years   b. 2000 years   c. 3000 years   d. 4000 years

27. How many years did it take archaeologists to catalogue every treasure in Tutankhamun's tomb?
a. 1 year   b. 4 years   c. 10 years   d. 25 years

28. What is the name of the most prominent Egyptian temple, still standing today, built in honour of Amun-Ra?
a. The Karnak temple complex   b. The Bolrock temple complex
c. The Amun temple complex   d. The Suridak temple complex

29. The Egyptians believed writing was a gift from which God?
a. Seth   b. Thoth   c. Ptah   d. Ra

30. Why were pictures often carved next to hieroglyphics?

31. What was the first capital of Ancient Egypt?
a. Alexandria   b. Memphis   c. Thebes

32. Where does the word hieroglyphic come from?
a. Romans   b. Ancient Greece   c. Ancient India   d. Ancient China

33. How many gods and goddesses did the Egyptians worship?
a. More than 500   b. More than 1000   c. More than 1500   d. More than 2000

34. Why were no mummies found in the Pyramids of Giza?

35. What was the main religion of Ancient Egypt?
a. Judaism   b. Buddhism   c. Polytheism   d. Hinduism

36. Which year was the Great Pyramid finished?
a. 3250 BCE   b. 2864 BCE   c. 2566 BCE   d. 2243 BCE

37. Which female pharaoh reigned the longest?
a. Cleopatra   b. Sobekneferu   c. Hatshepsut   d. Merneith

38. The Great Sphinx of Giza shows the head of the pharaoh Khafre on the body of which animal?
a. Rhino   b. Lion   c. Elephant   d. Giraffe

39. What did Pharaoh Pepi II allegedly cover his slaves in, in order to attract flies away from him?

40. How many children did Tutankhamun have?
a. 0   b. 1   c. 2   d. 3

41. What is the 'Curse of the Pharaohs' also known as the 'Curse of the Mummys'?

42. The Nile was vital to life in Ancient Egypt, but just how long is it?
a. 4890 km   b. 6650 km   c. 7910 km   d. 9050 km

43. Which god did the Egyptians believe would judge their soul when they died?

44. What powerful tribe from the Eastern Mediterranean did the Ancient Egyptians have to fight off?
a. Himba   b. Huli   c. Karo   d. Hitties

45. The scarab, placed inside the deceased's tomb, is shaped like which animal?

46. What is the name of the person who first managed to decipher Egyptian hieroglyphics?
a. Pierre-Simon Laplace   b. Antoine-Augustin Parmentier
c. Jean-François Champollion   d. Émilie du Châtelet

47. Which pharaoh changed the religion of Egypt from the worship of the god Amun to the worship of Aten?

48. The builders of the pyramids are said to have transported the granite from the quarries to the construction site by what method?

49. What was the name of the first pyramid to be built?
a. Pyramid of Meidum   b. Pyramid of Djoser   c. Pyramid of Menkaure

50. True or false: both Egyptian men and women wore makeup and perfume.

ANCIENT GREECE

1. In the Peloponnesian War, who was the enemy of Athens?

2. The first modern Olympian was held when?
a. 1834   b. 1856   c. 1862   d. 1896

3. At the Battle of Marathon, which Persian king did the Greeks defeat?

4. Where was Alexander the Great from?
a. Macedonia   b. Kosovo   c. Bulgaria   d. Albania

5. How did Socrates die?
a. Choking   b. Fell off a horse   c. Strangled in his sleep   d. Poisoning

6. Who won the Peloponnesian War?

7. In Greek mythology what was the name of the God of fire?
a. Hades   b. Aphrodite   c. Hephaestus   d. Hermes

8. Who was the ruler of Athens during the so-called 'Golden Age'?
a. Socrates   b. Pericles   c. Alexander the Great   d. Archelaos

9. What always happened on the third day of the Ancient Olympic games?
a. The sacrifice of 100 oxen to Zeus
b. 50 men were made to fight to the death to honour Ares
c. 10 slaves were selected to drink a broth, 5 of which contained poison, as a sacrifice to Hades

10. Which city did Alexander the Great siege in 332 BC?

11. Who was the ruler of the Titans?
a. Crius   b. Iapetus   c. Cronus   d. Rhea

12. According to Greek mythology, where did the 12 Olympians reside?

13. What was the prize for the winners of the Olympic Games in Ancient Greek times?
a. Gold medal   b. An olive wreath   c. Eternal wealth   d. Their own temple

14. In the Greek alphabet, what is the last letter?
a. Rho   b. Omicron   c. Zeta   d. Omega

15. What was the Goddess of war's name in Ancient Greece?

16. How many Gods and Goddesses lived on Mount Olympus?
a. 4   b. 8   c. 12   d. 16

17. What did the Greeks actually call themselves?

18. What small stringed toy are the Greeks believed to have invented?

19. What is the name of the most famous Greek temple, which was dedicated to the goddess Athena during the fifth century BC?

20. True or false: athletes regularly competed naked at the Ancient Olympic Games, in order to show Zeus their physical power.

21. What type of Greek monster was Cerberus?

22. How old were boys in Sparta when they started their training to defend the city?
a. 7 years old   b. 10 years old   c. 13 years old   d. 16 years old

23. Plato founded the Platonist school of thought and the Academy, but who was his teacher and mentor?

24. In Greek Mythology, the Trojan war was between who?

25. Who was the ruler of the Greek Gods?

26. This Ancient Greek is the author of two epic poems called Iliad and the Odyssey and is considered to be one of the most influential authors in history. What is his name?

27. What is the name of the league, founded in 478 BC, which was created to protect the Greeks against Spartan aggression? It was led by Athens and its powerful navy.

28. When is the traditional date for the end of Ancient Greece?
a. 300 BC   b. 323 BC   c. 340 BC   d. 363 BC

29. What were the tunics called that people wore during Ancient Greece?

30. From which alphabet did the Greek alphabet derive?

31. What did Eros' golden arrow make people do?

32. Which of the following is the Greek god of harvest?
a. Demeter   b. Dionysus   c. Artemis   d. Hera

33. True or false: women were not allowed to vote in the Ancient Greek democratic system.

34. Aphrodite was the Goddess of what?
a. Beuty and love   b. Sense and reason   c. Jealousy   d. Curiosity

35. What animal guards the entrance to the Ancient Greek city Mycenae?
a. Centaur   b. Gorgon   c. Lion   d. Bear

36. Which of the following people was not a famous playwright in Ancient Greece?
a. Euripides   b. Sophocles   c. Iasonas   d. Aeschylus

37. Who was the father of the Olympian gods?
a. Zeus   b. Jupiter   c. Uranus   d. Poseidon

38. Name the Ancient Greek playwright who wrote the play Antigone.
a. Sophocles   b. Aristophanes   c. Aeschylus   d. Plautus

39. This great Greek philosopher, born in 384 BC, was the student of Plato. One of his key works was on the subject of Nicomachean Ethics. What is his name?

40. Athens is known as the birthplace of what?
a. Communism   b. Democracy   c. Monarchy   d. Aristocracy

41. On which hill in Athens is the Parthenon located?

42. This Greek mathematician is considered to be the 'father of geometry'. He is the author of arguably the most successful mathematical textbook in history called Elements. What is his name?
a. Pythagoras   b. Euclid   c. Fermat   d. Archimedes

43. Name the Ancient Greek physician and 'father of modern medicine', who has an oath named after him which is still widely used today.

44. What were the Ancient Greek warships called, which were long narrow ships capable of reaching speeds of up to 9 knots?
a. Quinquereme   b. Triremes   c. Langskip   d. Felucca

45. What was a phalanx?
a. A military formation   b. A sword   c. The Greek word for trading   d. A traitor

46. Why did the Ancient Greeks not eat beans?
a. They believed they were poisonous
b. They were only for royalty
c. They believed that they caused you to age prematurely
d. They believed they contained the souls of the dead

47. The Ancient Greeks predominantly used two types of architecture. Which two of the following were they?
a. Doric   b. Baroque   c. Mughal   d. Ionic

48. Name the person who ran from Marathon to Athens to give news of the victory of the Battle of Marathon, who now has the prestigious race named after him.
a. Pheidippides   b. Solon   c. Herodotus

49. Which modern-day greeting did the ancient Greeks invent?

50. What is the name of the master carpenter who built the Trojan Horse?
a. Epeius   b. Atticus   c. Theo   d. Calliope

 # CELTIC BRITAIN

1. Who did the Celtic tribes sign a peace treaty with in 335 BC?

2. What were the branch of Celts that lived in Britain called?
a. Saxons   b. Jutes   c. Gaelic   d. Brythonic

3. There were approximately 16 Celtic languages to have ever existed. Six are still spoken today. Five of these are Irish, Manx, Scottish Gaelic, Breton, and Cornish, but what is the sixth?

4. What age did the Celts live in?
a. Stone Age   b. Bronze Age   c. Iron Age   d. Mesopotamia

5. What was the main religion of the Celts in Britain?
a. Christianity   b. Polytheism   c. Druidism   d. Paganism

6. What was a druid?

a. A member of the high-ranking class who was religious leaders

b. Someone who was outcast from the church for offending the gods

c. Common members of the church, resigned to a life of silence

7. In which year did the Romans conquer Britain, causing the Celts to slowly be subjugated and 'Romanized?

a. 95 AD   b. 67 AD   c. 43 AD   d. 19 AD

8. The Roman Empire, which ruled much of southern Europe at that time, referred to the Celts as "Galli," what does this mean?

a. Animals   b. Barbarians   c. Peasants   d. Farmers

9. Which of the following was the Celtic goddess of fertility and motherhood?

a. Mora   b. Belu   c. Firda   d. Danu

10. Where did the Celts come from?

a. Western Asia   b. Northern Africa   c. Central and Eastern Europe

11. Who were the Celts often in conflict with?

a. Romans   b. Egyptians   c. Greeks   d. Mongol Empire

12. How many gods is the Celtic religion thought to have had?

a. 1   b. 2   c. 50   d. 300

13. Which of the following is the Celtic Triskele?

a.   b.   c.    d.

14. Which Celtic Queen led a bloody revolt against the Romans?

a. Queen Brianna   b. Queen Boudica   c. Queen Maddox   d. Queen Rowan

15. To which tribe did the Queen from question 14 belong?

a. Caledones   b. Iceni   c. Venicones   d. Damnonii

THE ROMANS

1. According to tradition, when was Rome founded?
a. 753 BC   b. 780 BC   c. 802 BC   d. 838 BC

2. Who was the first Roman emperor?

3. What language was spoken by the Romans?

4. Which Emperor split the Roman Empire into two parts, the Western Empire including Rome, and the Eastern Empire including Constantinople? He did this because the Empire was becoming too large to rule effectively.

5. Who was the Roman God of the Sky and Thunder?
a. Saturn   b. Uranus   c. Mars   d. Jupiter

6. Under which Emperor did Christianity become the main religion of the Roman Empire?
a. Emperor Otho   b. Emperor Claudius
c. Emperor Galba   d. Emperor Constantine

7. How many hills was the ancient city of Rome built on?
a. 2   b. 5   c. 7   d. 10

8. On the Ides of March, Caesar was killed. What exact day in March was this?
a. 10th   b. 15th   c. 21st   d. 30th

9. According to tradition, which two brothers founded Rome?

10. What is the Colosseum in Rome also called?

11. Which Roman god was the God of the Underworld?

12. In which year was the Roman Colosseum finished being built?
a. 112 BC   b. 42 BC   c. 38 AD   d. 80 AD

13. What was the name of the important road that connected Rome to Brindisi, in southeast Italy?

14. Circus Maximus was once the first and largest stadium in ancient Rome. What was it primarily used for?
a. Chariot races and gladiatorial displays   b. Speeches from the Emperor
c. Public hangings and stoning   d. It acted as a public court

15. What is the Latin word for Gladiator?
a. Glerus   b. Gladius   c. Gladiturbus   d. Glamdius

16. Which Roman general and rival of Pompey defeated the slave revolt led by Spartacus?
a. Trajan   b. Commodus   c. Crassus   d. Valerian

17. The Pisonian conspiracy was a plot against which Emperor?
a. Augustus   b. Tiberius   c. Caligula   d. Nero

18. What is the name of the Roman Emperor who made his horse a senator?

19. Sundays were made the Roman day of rest by which Emporer in the year 321 AD?
a. Constantine I   b. Titus   c. Leo I   d. Marcian

20. Which of the following was the name of the Roman currency?
a. Denarius   b. Sickles   c. Fierius   d. Balarius

21. What name was given to the standard tactical unit of a Roman legion?

22. Who was the Roman God of War?
a. Ra   b. Mars   c. Apollo   d. Venus

23. What was the name of the author who wrote the famous poem Aeneid?
a. Cicero   b. Horace   c. Virgil   d. Livy

24. Which of the following was the last wife of Julius Caesar?
a. Agrippina the Younger   b. Orenus   c. Calpurnia   d. Valeria

25. An ancient roman road linked the places of Gloucester to Cirencester to Silchester. What was the name of this road?
a. Ermin Way   b. Biral's Road   c. Heron Street

26. Julius Ceasar was assassinated by a group of about 60 people because there were concerns that Caesar's excessive accumulation of authority during his rule as dictator was weakening the Roman Republic. Who were this group of 60 people?
a. Peasants   b. Senators   c. Monks   d. Scottish fighters

27. How many times was Julius Caesar stabbed?
a. 1 time   b. 12 times   c. 23 times   d. 54 times

28. Which of the following was the name of the Roman Empire's secret police?
a. Centurions   b. Praetorian Guard   c. Gladii   d. Frumentarii

29. Who was the Roman goddess of love and beauty?
a. Diana   b. Venus   c. Pandora   d. Maria

30. Which of the following are the names of the two famous walls built in Britain by the Romans?
a. Hadrian   b. Hadrada   c. Flavian   d. Trajanic   e. Antonine

31. Which city in the Roman Empire was destroyed by a volcano?

32. Who fought in the Battle of Cannae?

33. Constantine I introduced something called the solidus to Rome. What was this?
a. Coin   b. Sword   c. A type of punishment   d. Taxes

34. The period of peace and prosperity in Ancient Rome stretching from 27 BC - 180 AD was called what?

35. Which of the following was the Roman goddess of wisdom and warfare?
a. Venus   b. Minerva   c. Nimphedora   d. Deloria

36. Gaius Caesar was later given the nickname Caligula, which was a childhood nickname given to him by the soldiers of his father. What does Caligula actually mean?
a. Lion heart   b. Little boot   c. Small fish   d. Strange man

37. What was the primary responsibility of a Praetorian Guard?

38. Which Roman emperor became the founder of the Flavian dynasty?
a. Tiberius   b. Claudius   c. Nero   d. Vespasian

39. Who was the Roman God of the Sea?

40. What is the earliest written legislation of Ancient Roman law called?
a. Law of the Round Table   b. Law of the Ten Nobles
c. Law of the Twelve Tables   d. Law of the Commoners

41. In the Battle of Mursa, known as the 'bloodiest battle of the century', who did Constantius II defeat?

42. Who was the Emperor when Jesus was crucified?
a. Julius Caesar   b. Nero   c. Caligula   d. Trajan

43. What is the name of the famous church built under the direction of Justinian I?
a. Hagia Sophia   b. Dura-Europos   c. Santa Maria Maggiore

44. In the Code of Justinian, how many books are there?
a. 4   b. 7   c. 9   d. 12

45. What was the name of the privileged social class in Ancient Roman society?
a. Plebeians   b. Aristians   c. Patricians   d. Elecians

46. Which of the following was the name of the area where public meetings and markets were held?
a. The Commune   b. The Gathering   c. The Meeting   d. The Forum

47. Pontius Pilate allegedly ordered the crucifixion of which person?

48. What book on Stoic philosophy is Marcus Aurelius best known for writing?
a. Medea   b. Apology   c. The Meditations   d. The Twelve Caesars

49. When did Julius Caesar die?
a. 44 BCE   b. 48 BCE   c. 52 BCE   d. 55 BCE

50. The gladiator Spartacus led the third and largest slave revolt against Rome. What was the name of this war?

THE ANGLO-SAXONS

1. Which group of people invaded England in 1066?
a. The Greeks   b. The Normans   c. The Germans   d. The Vikings

2. Which period did the Anglo-Saxon era span?
a. 410-1066 AD   b. 345-1088 AD   c. 560-1094 AD   d. 530-1066 AD

3. What is the name of the final Anglo-Saxon King?

4. At which battle did this King lose his life?

5. Where did most Anglo-Saxons come from?
a. Italy   b. Poland   c. Russia   d. Germany

6. What language did the Anglo-Saxons speak?
a. Saxon   b. Old English   c. Celtic   d. Latin

7. Name the epic poem which was produced between 975 and 1025, in which the main character (whose name is the name of the poem) defeats a dragon but is mortally wounded in the process.

8. What is the name of the King who defeated the Vikings in the Battle of Edington in 878?
a. Edward the Great   b. Henry the Great
c. Alfred the Great   d. Harold the Great

9. What were the three biggest Anglo-Saxon tribes?
a. Jutes   b. Brigantes   c. Caereni   d. Angles   e. Ancalites   f. Saxons

10. What is the name of the Norman conqueror of England, who was victorious at the Battle of Hastings?

11. What were the religious beliefs of the Anglo-Saxons?

12. What was the name of the system of writing used by the Anglo-Saxons?
a. Cuneiform   b. Braille   c. Runic script   d. Elamite script

13. In what year did Edward the Confessor become King of England?
a. 884 AD   b. 935 AD   c. 988 AD   d. 1042 AD

14. Britain was divided into 5 different kingdoms. Four were Northumbria, Mercia, Kent, and East Anglia, but what was the fifth one?

15. What is the Anglo-Saxon word for 'king'? (hint - it derives from the Germanic word for King)

THE VIKINGS

1. Which area of the world did the Vikings come from?
a. North Asia   b. Scandinavia   c. The Caribbean   d. Southern Europe

2. What period did the Viking era span?
a. 584 - 1023   b. 704 - 988   c. 639 - 1123   d. 793 - 1066

3. What was the Viking name for a longship, which they used for raiding and exploration?
a. Bireme   b. Drakkar   c. Knoll   d. Birror

4. This Norse explorer is thought to be the first European person to set foot in continental America. Who is he?

5. What is the name of the supreme God that the Vikings worshipped?
a. Odin   b. Loki   c. Poseidon   d. Cleo

6. Thor, the God of war and fertility, used what weapon to create thunder and lightning?

7. In roughly which century did most of the Vikings convert to Christianity?
a. 11th-century   b. 9th-century   c. 13th-century   d. 14th-century

8. Jarls, the noble class, were buried in what?
a. Their houses   b. Tombs   c. Longships   d. Church cemetery

9. What is meant by the term Valhalla?

10. This world-famous Viking, born in 950, most likely earned his name 'the Red' due to the colour of his beard and hair. Who was he?

11. Which type of bird featured on the flags of Vikings?
a. Crow   b. Eagle   c. Hawk   d. Raven

12. Led by Ingolfur Arnarson, The Vikings settled in Iceland. In which year did they settle here?
a. 793 AD   b. 874 AD   c. 934 AD   d. 959 AD

13. How many classes was the Viking society divided into?
a. 3   b. 5   c. 7   d. 10

14. What language did the Vikings speak?
a. Anatolian   b. Ugaritic   c. Old Norse   d. Etruscan

15. This person ruled as the King of Denmark from 958 – 986. He shares his surname with a short-range wireless technology.

THE MONGOL EMPIRE

1. The Mongol Empire was founded in 1206, who founded the empire?

2. At the empire's peak, how many square miles of territory did it cover?
a. 2 million square miles   b. 5 million square miles
c. 6 million square miles   d. 9 million square miles

3. How many people today are thought to be descendants of Genghis Khan?
a. 1 million   b. 16 million   c. 104 million   d. 285 million

4. Which of the following was the capital of the Mongol Empire?
a. Hong Kong   b. Karakorum   c. Ayutthaya   d. Luang Prabang

5. There were two main religions within the Mongol Empire. Which of the following were they?
a. Taoism   b. Tengrism   c. Christianity   d. Buddhism   e. Confucianism

6. In which year did Genghis Khan die?
a. 1217   b. 1227   c. 1237   d. 1247

7. In which year did the Mongol Empire fall?
a. 1368   b. 1397   c. 1451   d. 1499

8. True or false: the Mongol Empire is considered to be the largest Empire by area in history.

9. What was the primary weapon that was used by the Mongols?
a. Swords   b. Spears   c. Catapult   d. Bow and arrow

10. The Mongol Empire was too large to maintain and broke into multiple parts, with each part being ruled by its own Khan. What were these parts called?

THE OTTOMAN EMPIRE

1. When was the Ottoman Empire founded?
a. 1299   b. 1365   c. 1473   d. 1539

2. How many Sultans ruled the Ottoman Empire?
a. 1   b. 2   c. 12   d. 36

3. What was the capital of the Ottoman Empire?
a. Ankara   b. Athens   c. Istanbul   d. Podgorica

4. Who was the founder of the Ottoman Empire?
a. Hamid II   b. Osman I   c. Adem I   d. Ayaz II

5. What was the primary religion of the Ottoman Empire?
a. Buddhism   b. Hinduism   c. Christianity   d. Islam

6. The Ottomans conquered Constantinople in 1453, which sultan lead this?
a. Berat   b. Eymen II   c. Mehmed II   d. Hamza III

7. In which country did the Ottoman Empire start? Bonus point if you guess the city!
a. Greece   b. Turkey   c. Armenia   d. Albania

8. Why did the Ottoman Empire end?

9. The Ottoman Empire was known as the "Sick man of Europe". Why?

10. In which year did the Ottoman Empire end?
a. 1922   b. 1932   c. 1942   d. 1952

THE AZTECS

1. What did the Aztecs sacrifice to their Gods?
a. The human brain   b. The large intestine   c. A still-beating human heart

2. Which modern-day country did the Aztecs live in?
a. Peru   b. Mexico   c. Venezuela   d. Colombia

3. What were the Aztecs also known as?

4. What is the Aztec language called?
a. Nahuatl   b. Tenuatl   c. Aztuatl   d. Menuatl

5. To defeat their most powerful rivals, the Aztecs formed a three-way alliance with the Texocans and the Tacubans. In which year did they form the alliance?
a. 1323   b. 1368   c. 1404   d. 1428

6. When did the Aztec Empire end?
a. 1492   b. 1521   c. 1546   d. 1569

7. Who was the Aztec God of War?
a. Huitzilopochtli   b. Xipe   c. Totec   d. Tezcatlipoca

8. What was the name of the last Aztec emperor?
a. Huitzilihuitl   b. Itzcoatl   c. Tizoc   d. Cuauhtémoc

9. Which European power eventually overthrew the Aztec Empire?

10. Which disease had a devastating outbreak for the Aztecs following the arrival of the Europeans, allowing them to easily take the capital city?
a. Black death   b. Smallpox   c. Typhus   d. Cholera

11. Which of the following was the most important food for the Aztecs?
a. Grain   b. Wheat   c. Barley   d. Maize

12. Tlaloc was the Aztec God of what?
a. War and Thunder   b. The Afterlife
c. Rain and Fertility   d. Love and Friendship

13. What was the capital of the Aztec empire?
a. Texcoco   b. Tlacopan   c. Tenochtitlan

14. What industry did the Aztec economy revolve around?
a. Raiding and pillaging   b. Fishing   c. Mining   d. Agriculture and trading

15. What was the reason for their human sacrifices?
a. To punish criminals   b. To have good luck with the harvest
c. To get rid of the weak   d. To please the gods

THE RENAISSANCE

1. Where is the birthplace of the Renaissance?
a. Florence, Italy   b. Rome Italy   c. Barcelona, Spain   d. Budapest, Hungary

2. What is the name of the family which ruled this city for more than 60 years?

3. The Renaissance period saw the birth of some of the most famous intellectuals. What is the name of the Italian artist who painted the 'Mona Lisa'?

4. What does the word Renaissance mean?
a. Culture   b. Art   c. Rebirth   d. Awakening

5. When did the Renaissance period begin?
a. 14th century   b. 15th century   c. 16th century   d. 17th century

6. Which of the following is considered to be the father of the Renaissance?
a. Francesco Petrarca   b. Lorenzo de' Medici   c. Nicolaus Copernicus

7. What was the main philosophy during the Renaissance period?
a. axiology   b. Brahmoism   c. Deism   d. Humanism

8. What was the height of the Renaissance period called?
a. Peak Renaissance   b. High Renaissance
c. Holy Renaissance   d. Eternal Renaissance

9. What is the name of the Italian artist who painted the Sistine Chapel ceiling?
a. Leonardo da Vinci   b. Donatello   c. Raphael   d. Michelangelo

10. What new form of Christianity was created during the Renaissance period?

11. When did the Renaissance period end?
a. 14th century   b. 16th century   c. 17th century   d. 18th century

12. What did Johannes Gutenberg invent in 1450, which would change the world as they knew it?

13. Name the Italian diplomat, author and philosopher who wrote The Prince which was published in 1532.
a. Giovanni Boccaccio   b. Niccolò Machiavelli   c. Edmund Spenser

14. This Italian astronomer, physicist and philosopher is considered to be the father of modern Physics. His discoveries about the Moon, Jupiter's moons, Venus and sunspots supported the idea that the Earth was not the centre of the universe, but rather the sun was. Who is he?

15. What is the name of the most valuable painting to come from the Renaissance period?

16. This man was one of the most prominent philosophers of the French Renaissance. He is known for creating the essay style of writing, and his massive volume Essais contained some of the most influential essays ever written. What is his name?

17. What was the name of the plague that swept through Europe during the Renaissance period?

18. Which famous English poet and playwriter who wrote "Romeo and Juliet" existed in the Renaissance period?

19. What famous explorer discovered America and discarded the theory of the world being flat during this era?

20. What type of art was Donatello best known for?
a. Painting   b. Mosaic   c. Drawing   d. Sculptures

THE INCA EMPIRE

1. What is the name of the Inca citadel located in southern Peru, often referred to as the "Lost City of the Incas"?

2. In which century was this citadel built?
a. 14th-century   b. 15th-century   c. 16th-century   d. 17th-century

3. Which area did the Inca Empire originate from?

4. At its peak how many inhabitants did the Inca Empire consist of?
a. 4 million   b. 7 million   c. 12 million   d. 15 million

5. It took the Spanish 40 years to fully conquer the last Inca state after they began their conquest. In which year did they conquer this final state?
a. 1484   b. 1521   c. 1547   d. 1572

6. Apu Illapu, was the God of what?
a. Harvest   b. Thunder   c. Reproduction   d. Rain

7. What was the capital of the Inca Empire?
a. Ollantaytambo   b. Pisac   c. Ingapirca   d. Cuzco

8. What was the name of the founder of the Inca dynasty?
a. Manco Capac   b. Amaru Atoc   c. Mama Quilla   d. Capac Yupanqui

9. The Inca people's clothing was made from the wool of which animal?
a. Sheep   b. Goats   c. Oxen   d. Llamas and alpacas

10. What was the main language spoken by the Incas?
a. Spanish   b. Aymaran   c. Quechua   d. Tupí-Guaraní

11. What is the name of the great creator deity in Inca mythology?

a. Viracocha   b. Pacha Mama   c. Inti   d. Supay

12. True or false: the Inca Empire had a centralised government, with all states operating under the same laws.

13. The Inca Empire is known for its impressive road network. How many miles did the road network run?

a. 10,000 miles   b. 25,000 miles   c. 50,000 miles   d. 90,000 miles

14. The Inca had a system of record-keeping known as quipu. What material did they use for their system of record-keeping?

15. When was the Inca Empire founded?

a. 1378   b. 1399   c. 1418   d. 1438

THE TUDORS

1. Who did Henry VII defeat at the Battle of Bosworth in 1485 to become the first Tudor King?
a. Richard II   b. Edward V   c. Edward IV   d. Richard III

2. What were the names of the two wives Henry VIII had beheaded?

3. What age was Edward VI when he became king?
a. 9   b. 11   c. 13   d. 15

4. What was the name of the famous theatre where Shakespeare's plays were performed?
a. The Performance Theatre   b. The Royal Theatre
c. The Globe Theatre   d. Convent Garden Theatre

5. What nickname was given to Queen Mary?

6. In which year was Mary Queen of Scots executed?
a. 1567   b. 1577   c. 1587   d. 1597

7. What is the name of the Welsh castle where Henry VII was born?
a. Cardiff Castle   b. Pembroke Castle   c. Caernarfon Castle   d. Harlech Castle

8. Henry VII married Elizabeth of York which united the House of Plantagenet with which other house?
a. House of Wessex   b. House of York
c. House of Windsor   d. House of Lancaster

9. Elizabeth I was sometimes known by which other name?

10. Lady Jane Grey was the titular queen of England for how long?
a. 9 hours   b. 9 days   c. 9 weeks   d. 9 months

11. What was the name of the principal advisor of Henry VIII who was executed in 1540 for treason and heresy?
a. Guy Fairfax   b. Thomas Fich   c. Thomas Barowe   d. Thomas Cromwell

12. What happened to Thomas Cranmer, the archbishop of Canterbury during the Tudor period?
a. Burnt at the stake for heresay
b. Beheaded for attempting to kill Henry VIII
c. Banished from England for treason
d. Imprisoned for false accusations

13. Which woman did Henry VIII marry which led to his break with the Roman Catholic Church?

14. What was the name of the famous artist who was Henry VIII's personal Painter?

15. "The Lamentations of a Sinner" is a three-part sequence of reflections. Which of Henry VIII's wives wrote this?
a. Anne Boleyn   b. Catherine Parr   c. Catherine of Aragon

16. Thomas More was Chancellor to Henry VIII. What was the name of the book he published in 1516?

17. What was the name of the emblem of England during the Tudor period?
a. Tudor Lilly   b. Tudor Rose   c. Tudor Shield   d. Tudor Hammer

18. Who were the richest and most powerful people of Tudor times?
a. Priests   b. Archbishops   c. Farmers   d. Monks

19. How many times did Henry VIII marry?
a. 4 times   b. 5 times   c. 6 times   d. 7 times

20. What was the common punishment for stealing during Tudor times?
a. Whipping   b. Monetary fines
c. Community service   d. Public walk of shame

21. In which year did the Tudor period begin?
a. 1450   b. 1463   c. 1485   d. 1490

22. How many Tudor monarchs were there?
a. 3   b. 6   c. 9   d. 12

23. Why did Henry VIII divorce Catherine of Aragon?
a. He believed she was being unfaithful
b. He believed she could not give him a son
c. He believed her religious beliefs comprised his position as king

24. After how many months did Henry VIII and Anne of Cleves get divorced?
a. 2 months   b. 4 months   c. 6 months   d. 8 months

25. In 1512 Henry VIII banned ordinary people from doing what?
a. Music   b. Art   c. Sport   d. Acting

26. Why did it become fashionable to have blackened teeth from sugar during the Tudor times?

27. What was the average life expectancy of people in the Tudor times?
a. 25- 30 years   b. 30-35 years   c. 35-40 years   d. 45-50 years

28. What is the name of the rebellion led by Robert Aske against Henry VII?

29. Myles Coverdale published the first authorised and complete Modern English edition of which book in 1535?

30. Who was the final Tudor monarch?

31. Pope Leo X awarded Henry VIII which title in 1521?
a. Defender of the People   b. Defender of the Realm   c. Defender of the Faith

32. In which year did the "Prayer Book Rebellion" take place?
a. 1529   b. 1549   c. 1569   d. 1589

33. How many years did the "War of the Roses" span?
a. 12 years   b. 22 years   c. 32 years   d. 42 years

34. What is the name of Henry's most famous ship?
a. The Mayflower   b. The Mary Rose   c. The Cutty Sark   d. HMS Victory

35. Who was the main architect commissioned to build Hampton Court Palace?
a. Robert Hamley   b. Nicholas Williams   c. Christopher Wren   d. James Ogle

36. What type of colourful bird was a popular dish at a Tudor feast?
a. Kingfisher   b. Golden Pheasant   c. Mandarin Duck   d. Peacock

37. Elizabeth I's reign was a time when power, art, and culture thrived. What was this time of reign also known as?

38. What was the name of the explorer who sailed to North America in 1497 on behalf of Henry VII and laid the foundations of the English Empire there?
a. Walter Raleigh   b. Martin Frobisher   c. John Cabot   d. John Hawkins

39. In which year was William Shakespeare born?
a. 1564   b. 1578   c. 1592   d. 1608

40. London Bridge was a place where traitors' heads were displayed on sticks. What crime was this warning people not to commit?
a. Murder   b. Treason   c. Adultery   d. Monogamy

THE NAPOLEONIC WARS

1. In which battle did Napoleon face his final defeat?

2. In which year was Napoleon Bonaparte born?
a. 1759   b. 1769   c. 1779   d. 1789

3. In 1812 Napoleon lead an invasion of Russia in which his army was forced to retreat. What was the name of this battle?
a. Battle of Abukir   b. Battle of Cadiz   c. Battle of Borodino

4. Napoleon was exiled on two occasions. Which island was he exiled to the second time?

5. At what age did Napoleon die?
a. 44   b. 51   c. 58   d. 63

6. Who commanded the British Army to victory in 1815?

7. In which year was Napoleon exiled to Elba, an island off the coast of Italy?
a. 1808   b. 1814   c. 1820   d. 1825

8. What does the expression 'met your Waterloo' mean today?

9. Napoleon fought in 43 listed battles, how many of these did he win?
a. 12   b. 22   c. 32   d. 38

10. In which year did Napoleon become the Emperor of France?
a. 1804   b. 1809   c. 1814   d. 1820

11. What was Napoleon also known as?

a. The Little Corporal   b. The Tiny Leader

c. The Small Ruler   d. The Pocket Master

12. What was the name of Napoleon's first campaign back after escaping exile?

a. The 10 Days   b. The 50 Days   c. The 100 Days   d. The 200 Days

13. England, Spain, and which other country fought against France in the Peninsular War?

a. Germany   b. Portugal   c. Austria   d. Belgium

14. The Fifth Coalition battle between England and Austria against France began in which year?

a. 1802   b. 1809   c. 1815   d. 1820

15. What is Napoleon likely to have died from?

a. Heart attack   b. Poisoning   c. Choking   d. Stomach cancer

AMERICAN CIVIL WAR

1. Roughly what percentage of the US population died in the American civil war?
a. 2%   b. 4%   c. 6%   d. 8%

2. Which battle had the most casualties?
a. Battle of Fort Sumter   b. Battle of Shiloh
c. Battle of Chickamauga   d. Battle of Gettysburg

3. Which era followed the American Civil War?

4. Who was the commander of the Union army during the Civil War?

5. A semi-military secret organisation was running in the Midwestern states during the American Civil War, what was the name of the organisation?
a. Knights of the Round Table   b. Knights of the Golden Circle
c. Knights of the Holy Hour   d. Knights of the People's Protectors

6. Robert E. Lee used one horse through most of the civil war, what was the name of this horse?
a. Voyager   b. Traveller   c. Journeyman   d. Faithful

7. What was the name of the courthouse where General Robert E. Lee surrendered to Union General Ulysses S. Grant?
a. King William County Courthouse   b. Hanover County Courthouse
c. Richmond County Courthouse   d. Appomattox Court House

8. Nathan Bedford Forrest was the Confederate general in command at which massacre?
a. Fort Pillow Massacre   b. Gallinas massacre   c. Palmyra massacre

9. What was significant about the naval battle between the Merrimack and the Monitor?
a. It was the first naval battle of the war
b. It was the first battle with ironclad warships
c. It was the turning point of the war for the United States of America
d. It was the first battle with steel-clad warships

10. What was the name of the first successful rapid-fire repeating gun invented during the American Civil War?
a. Agar gun   b. Bailey machine gun   c. Colt machine gun   d. Gatling gun

11. How many states made up the Confederate States of America?
a. 10   b. 11   c. 12   d. 13

12. How many of these Confederate States can you name?

13. Who won the Battle of Gettysburg?
a. Confederate victory   b. Union victory   c. Neither side won

14. Stephen Vincent Benét published a poem about the American Civil War in 1928. What was the name of this poem?
a. Still I Rise   b. The Raven   c. Mock Orange   d. John Brown's Body

15. In which year was Abraham Lincoln assassinated?
a. 1863   b. 1864   c. 1865   d. 1866

16. What caused the American Civil War?

17. Who won the civil war?

18. What percentage of African Americans made up the Union army?
a. 5%   b. 10%   c. 15%   d. 20%

19. Belle Boyd was a spy for which side in the Civil War?

20. Who was the President of the Confederate States from 1861 - 1865?

21. Where did the American Civil War begin?

22. Which of the following was not a battle in the Civil War?
a. Battle of Chusto-Talasah   b. Battle of Harforough Sands
c. Battle of Dranesville   d. Battle of Cockpit Point

23. What was the name of the well-known 19th-century American photographer who was recognised for his photographs of the American Civil War?
a. Matthew Brady   b. James Smith   c. James Johnson   d. Richard Wilson

24. How many people are estimated to have died in the American Civil War
a. 620,000   b. 780,000   c. 970,000   d. 1,200,000

25. In which state did the south surrender?
a. Maine   b. Virginia   c. Ohio   d. Michigan

26. Who assassinated Abraham Lincoln?

27. What was Abraham Lincoln attending when he was assassinated?
a. A court hearing   b. A play   c. A school opening ceremony

28. What caused most of the deaths and casualties during the Civil War?

29. How long did the American Civil War last?
a. 3 years   b. 4 years   c. 5 years   d. 6 years

30. What name is the American Civil War also known as?

31. In which year was the Battle of Fort Donelson?
a. 1862   b. 1863   c. 1864   d. 1865

32. What is the name of the battle that took place at the River of Death?

a. Battle of Big Bethel   b. Battle of Rich Mountain

c. Battle of Chickamauga   d. Battle of Dry Wood Creek

33. True or false: after the Civil War, African American men were given the right to vote.

34. Who was the overall commander of the Confederate States at the end of the Civil War?

35. What was the name of the first submarine to sink an enemy ship during the American Civil War?

a. H.L. Hunley   b. H.L. Bentley   c. H.L. Furley   d. H.L. Plenley

COLONIALISM

1. Which territory in South America is still owned by the French?

2. In what century did what's known as *modern colonialism* or *The Age of Discovery* begin?
a. 14th century   b. 15th century   c. 16th century   d. 17th century

3. Which country committed the first genocide of the 20th century, in the country that is now known as Namibia?
a. Great Britain   b. Spain   c. Germany   d. France

4. In 1858 the British government directly ruled India. What did India then become known as?
a. British India   b. The British Republic   c. Little Britain   d. The British Raj

5. This war was fought in 1879 in what is now known as South Africa. The result was a British victory, and it ended with the partition of the Zulu Kingdom. What is the name of this war?

6. Which European country was the first to create colonies in Asia?
a. Spain   b. The Netherlands   c. Great Britain   d. Portugal

7. What is the name of the company that was formed to trade in the Indian Ocean region? It started with the East Indies but later moved to East Asia, eventually becoming the largest corporation in the world.
a. East India Company   b. North India Company
c. South Asia Company   d. West India Company

8. What Central American country was a British colony until the late 20th century?
a. Nicaragua   b. El Salvador   c. Guatemala   d. Belize

9. Which of the following Asian countries was never colonised?
a. Cambodia   b. Pakistan   c. Thailand   d. Vietnam

10. Which European country colonised Indonesia in the 1600s?

11. How many people speak French in Africa as a result of colonialism?
a. 141 million   b. 182 million   c. 242 million   d. 291 million

12. Dutch Ceylon existed from 1640 - 1796. Which modern-day country is this now?

13. What is the name of the popular Vietnamese snack which uses a French baguette and is filled with Vietnamese fillings?

14. Which African country changed its name to reject any colonial ties from the past in April 2018?

15. At its peak, how many people did the British Empire rule?
a. 310 million   b. 392 million   c. 458 million   d. 535 million

16. Natives of which island killed James Cook in 1779?

17. In which century did the second wave of colonisation take place?
a. 17th century   b. 18th century   c. 19th century   d. 20th century

18. What is the second wave of colonial expansion called?

19. Which Belgium King is known as "the Butcher of Congo" for his brutalist colonial regimes?
a. Louis I   b. Leopold I   c. Leopold II   d. Albert I

20. What significant event happened during the "Trail of Tears"?

21. The ABC islands are still owned by which European country?
a. The Netherlands   b. Belgium   c. France   d. Spain

22. The language Afrikaans is very similar to which European language due to colonisation?

23. What is the name of the indigenous people from Australia?

24. In which year was Australia colonised?
a. 1778   b. 1788   c. 1798   d. 1808

25. How many people lost their lives in the 1943 Bengal famine in India, largely due to the policies implemented by Churchill?
a. 1 million   b. 2 million   c. 3 million   d. 4 million

26. Zimbabwe was the last African country to gain independence from the British Empire. In which year did Zimbabwe gain independence?
a. 1970   b. 1980   c. 1990   d. 2000

27. During the second Boer War, the British detained about 107,000 people which were mainly women and children and put them in camps. How many of these people lost their lives?
a. 19,000   b. 28,000   c. 39,000   d. 47,000

28. Name the country which colonised the most countries.

29. In which year did the Bahamas gain independence from the British Empire?
a. 1953   b. 1963   c. 1973   d. 1983

30. Great Britain caused terrible atrocities during the Mau Mau uprising, with historians debating the death toll to be between 20,000 - 100,000. This country has now launched a £200 million damages claim against the UK government, but which country was this in?

WORLD WAR ONE

1. The Treaty of Neuilly was signed between the Allied Powers and which country?
a. Bulgaria   b. Romania   c. Slovenia   d. Italy

2. What year did World War 1 end?
a. 1915   b. 1916   c. 1917   d. 1918

3. Which disease was present during World War 1 that killed an estimation of 25 million people?

4. What was the association between Great Britain, France and Russia called?

5. Which year did the United States enter World War 1?
a. 1914   b. 1915   c. 1916   d. 1917

6. Mata Hari was convicted of doing what during World War 1?
a. Attempting to assassinate the British Prime Minister
b. Spying on Germany's behalf
c. Spying on America's behalf

7. Edith Cavell became a popular heroine during World War 1. What did she do?

8. This battle was fought from 21 February to 18 December 1916 on the Western Front in France. It was the longest battle of WWI, and also one of the deadliest. Which battle was this?

9. In which year did Italy switch sides and join the Allies?
a. 1915   b. 1916   c. 1917   d. 1918

10. The Third Battle of Ypres was also known as what?
a. Battle of Galicia   b. Battle of Krithia Vineyard   c. Battle of Passchendaele

11. What pattern were trenches dug in?
a. Straight lines   b. Zig-zags   c. Curves   d. Parallel rows

12. What was the name of the battle where the tank was first introduced?
a. Second Battle of Artois   b. Second Battle of Champagne
c. Hundred Days Offensive   d. Battle of the Somme

13. Who was the Prime Minister of the United Kingdom at the start of World War I?

14. What is the name of the last surviving American World War I veteran?
a. Bright Williams   b. Robley Rex   c. Frank Buckles   d. Brent Furley

15. Which country signed a treaty with the Central Powers, ending its participation in WWI, on March 3 1918?

16. The June Offensive was a desperate final effort from Russia to win the war. In which year did the June Offensive take place?
a. 1915   b. 1916   c. 1917   d. 1918

17. The Battle of Vittorio Veneto was a final victory for which country?

18. U.S. President Woodrow Wilson proposed a postwar peace organisation called the League of Nations. In which year did the US officially join the League of Nations?
a. 1918   b. 1919   c. 1924   d. They never did

19. Who was the German Kaiser during WWI?

20. Which controversial battle tactic was first used at the Second Battle of Ypres in 1915?
a. Dropping acid from planes   b. Poison gas   c. Poisoning the water supply

21. Which three countries were in the Triple Alliance?

22. What is the name of the peace treaty that was signed on 28 June 1919, which required Germany to pay financial reparations, disarm and lose territories?

23. What is the name of the gas, unleashed by the Germans in the summer of 1917, which attacked the skin and blinded its victims, rendering gas masks useless?
a. Mustard Gas   b. Mayonaise Gas   c. Honey Gas   d. Olive Oil Gas

24. Who was the US President during WW1?

25. What is meant by the term dogfights in WWI?

26. What day was Armistice Day?

27. Which type of bird was used to carry messages during WW1?
a. Crows   b. Ravens   c. Owls   d. Pigeons

28. The Red Baron was Germany's top aviator during WW1. How many enemy warcrafts did he shoot down?
a. 30   b. 50   c. 80   d. 150

29. What is the name of the Archduke of Austria who was assassinated in 1914, causing the start of World War I?

30. Who was the Prime Minister of the United Kingdom at the end of the war?

WORLD WAR TWO

1. How many Jews were killed during the Holocaust?
a. 4 million   b. 6 million   c. 8 million   d. 10 million

2. Which battle was the longest in WWII?
a. Battle of Moerbrugge   b. Battle of the Bulge
c. Leningrad–Novgorod Offensive   d. Battle of the Atlantic

3. What is the name of the most notorious Nazi concentration camp, which had the highest death toll in WWII?

4. Which country suffered the most casualties during WWII?
a. Germany   b. The Soviet Union   c. America   d. Great Britain

5. In which year did WWII start?
a. 1938   b. 1939   c. 1940   d. 1941

6. Which country did Hitler invade, causing Great Britain and France to declare war on Germany?

7. Which countries made up the Axis Alliance?

8. The D-day operation took place on June 6, 1944, and was one of the largest invasions in human history. Where did the invasion take place?

9. How did Adolf Hitler die?
a. A cyanide pill   b. Suicide by gunshot   c. An enemy explosion   d. Poisoning

10. How many years did WWII last?
a. 5 years   b. 6 years   c. 7 years   d. 8 years

11. Which man is credited with cracking the enigma code?

12. VE Day is held on 8th May each year. What does VE Day stand for?

13. The Allies included which five countries?

14. Why was the Battle of Britain so unique?
a. It was the first battle where U-Boats were used
b. It was the first battle with drone-controlled bombs
c. It was the first battle to be fought entirely by air forces

15. Who was the leader of the Soviet Union during World War II?
a. Vladimir Lenin   b. Joseph Stalin
c. Georgy Malenkov   d. Nikita Khrushchev

16. Who was the supreme commander of the Allied forces in western Europe during World War II?

17. On which date did America declare war on Imperial Japan, and therefore join the war?
a. December 18, 1940   b. March 22, 1941
c. July 02, 1941   d. December 07, 1941

18. What is the name of the chief propagandist of the Nazi Party who committed suicide on 1 May 1945 alongside his wife and six children?

19. Approximately how many soldiers fought on behalf of the Allied or Axis countries?
a. 30 million   b. 50 million   c. 70 million   d. 100 million

20. Switzerland, Spain, and Portugal all declared themselves neutral during WW2. Which of the following counties also declared themselves neutral?
a. Norway   b. Sweden   c. Finland   d. Denmark

21. In which country did the Battle of Dunkirk take place? 22. In 1940 and 1941 the United Kingdom experienced an intense bombing campaign from Germany. What was this called?

23. Which country won the battle of Midway?

24. Which Japanese city was the first nuclear bomb dropped on?
a. Hiroshima   b. Nagasaki

25. What is the name of the plane that dropped the second nuclear bomb?
a. Curtiss Hawk   b. Enola Gay
c. Armstrong Whitworth Scimitar   d. Hawker Fury

26. Who was the Prime Minister of the United Kingdom when WW2 ended?

27. Approximately how many American soldiers lost their lives in WWII?
a. 405,000   b. 588,000   c. 728,000   d. 918,000

28. Germany surrendered on May 7, 1945. When did Japan finally surrender?
a. September 02, 1945   b. October 28, 1945   c. December 02, 1945

29. Which Japanese admiral was behind the Pearl Harbour attack?

30. The Doolittle Raid was a US air raid which targeted major cities in which country?
a. Germany   b. Japan   c. Italy   d. Austria

31. In which year did the attack on Pearl Harbor take place?
a. 1940   b. 1941   c. 1942   d. 1943

32. What is the name of the second deadliest concentration camp in WWII, taking the lives of approximately 800,000 people?
a. Treblinka   b. Bełżec   c. Sobibór   d. Chełmno

33. Who was the US president when WW2 came to an end?

34. In which country was Auschwitz built?

35. The Molotov-Ribbentrop Pact was a non-aggression pact between Germany and which other country, that was signed the month before war broke out?

36. What is the name of the plan, signed on April 3, 1948, which proposed that the US provide economic help to help restore postwar Europe?

37. What was the name of the German submarine used during WW2?
a. Z-boat   b. U-boat   c. X-boat   d. Y-boat

38. What was the name of Hitler's wife?

39. Operation Overlord was the code name for which battle?
a. Battle of Kursk   b. Battle of Okinawa
c. Battle of Stalingrad   d. The Battle of Normandy

40. What is the name of the government research project that produced the first atomic bombs?
a. New York Project   b. Los Angeles Project
c. Manhattan Project   d. Boston Project

THE COLD WAR

1. What were the two main countries involved in the Cold War?

2. What does NATO stand for?

3. What was discussed in the Strategic Arms Limitation Talks?

4. On which island did an American U-2 spy plane photograph nuclear missile sites that were being built by the Soviet Union in October 1962?

5. What is the name of the military, political and ideological boundary created by the Soviet Union after the war to seal it and its Eastern and Central European allies from open contact with the West?
a. Steel Curtain   b. Wooden Curtain   c. Iron Curtain   d. Gold Curtain

6. The Western Block was the name of the respective allies for which country?

7. In which year did the Cold War begin?
a. 1946   b. 1947   c. 1949   d. 1951

8. What pact did the Soviet Union form in response to NATO in 1955?
a. Moscow Pact   b. Kazan Pact   c. Krakow Pact   d. Warsaw Pact

9. In 1948 the Berlin Blockade took place. What was the purpose of the Berlin Blockade?

10. Who was in charge of Cuba during the Cuban Missile Crisis?

11. U.S. diplomat George Kennan created the doctrine that formed the basis of U.S. foreign policy during the Cold War. What is the name of this doctrine?
a. Containment   b. Authority   c. Management   d. Restriction

12. How long did the Cuban Missile Crisis last?
a. 8 days   b. 13 days   c. 45 days   d. 3 months

13. In which year did China become a communist nation led by Mao Zedong?
a. 1949   b. 1951   c. 1953   d. 1955

14. In which year was NATO formed?
a. 1945   b. 1949   c. 1953   d. 1957

15. Name the writer who created the term 'cold war' in 1945?
a. T.S. Eliot   b. Ian Fleming   c. C.S. Lewis   d. George Orwell

16. In the 1970s the US created a policy approach that aimed to reduce tensions with the Soviet Union. What was the name of the policy?
a. Calmante   b. Rassurante   c. Détente   d. apaisement

17. In what year did the Fall of the Berlin Wall take place?
a. 1989   b. 1990   c. 1991   d. 1992

18. In which year did the Cold War come to an end?
a. 1989   b. 1991   c. 1993   d. 1995

19. Who was the leader of the Soviet Union when it collapsed?

20. Who was the leader of the United States when the Cold War came to an end?

21. What does the term Proxy war mean?

22. How long did the Cold War last?
a. 25 years   b. 35 years   c. 45 years   d. 55 years

23. How long did the Soviet-Afghan War last?
a. 4 years   b. 6 years   c. 9 years   d. 12 years

24. In which year did the USA detonate the world's first hydrogen bomb named Mike?
a. 1949   b. 1952   c. 1955   d. 1959

25. In which Eastern European country was there an uprising against the Soviets from 23 October 1956 – 11 November 1956?
a. Romania   b. Hungary   c. Bulgaria   d. Slovakia

THE KOREAN WAR

1. In which year did the Korean War start?
a. 1949 b. 1950 c. 1951 d. 1952

2. Which countries were on the side of North Korea?
a. China and the Soviet Union   b. The United States and the allied countries

3. In 1948 Korea was divided into sovereign states. How many states was Korea divided into?
a. 2 b. 4 c. 6 d. 8

4. The main reason for the Korean War was that the Americans wanted to stop the spread of which political ideology?

5. Which of the following was not a battle fought in the Korean War?
a. Battle of Kapyong   b. Battle of Chosin Reservoir
c. Battle of Pusan Perimeter d. Battle of Ia Drang

6. The Battle of Inchon was fought for four days in September in 1950. Which side came out as decisive winners at this battle?
a. The United States and allied nations   b. China and the Soviet Union

7. The Battle of Heartbreak Ridge took place in which year?
a. 1950   b. 1951   c. 1952   d. 1953

8. A line divides North Korea and South Korea, what is the name of this line?
a. 24th parallel   b. 32nd parallel   c. 38th parallel   d. 47th parallel

9. How many years did the Korean War last?
a. 2 years   b. 3 years   c. 5 years   d. 7 years

10. The Korean War began after which side invaded the other?

11. At the time of the war's outbreak, who was North Korea's leader?
a. Kim Jong-il   b. Kim Jun-woo   c. Kim Jong-un   d. Kim Il-sung

12. What percent of American prisoners of war died during the Korean War?
a. 6%   b. 19%   c. 30%   d. 38%

13. The Korean War was the first war to use air-to-air combat with which type of aircraft?
a. biplanes   b. Jet fighters   c. Helicopters   d. Spitfires

14. Which of the following people was the leader of South Korea during the Korean War?
a. Ho Chong   b. Rhee Syng-man   c. Paik Nak-chun   d. Kwak Sang-hoon

15. How many people died during the Korean War?
a. 1 million   b. 3 million   c. 5 million   d. 7 million

CIVIL RIGHTS

1. What is the name of the state and local laws introduced to the Southern United States in the late 19th and early 20th centuries that enforced racial segregation?

2. What was the name of the person who famously did not give up their seat to a white man in 1955?

3. Who led the Montgomery Improvement Association (MIA)?

4. What was The Montgomery Bus Boycott?

5. How many days did The Montgomery Bus Boycott last?
a. 81 days   b. 181 days   c. 281 days   d. 381 days

6. What name was given to the nine brave African-American students who arrived at their high school in Arkansas after the supreme court outlawed segregation, only to be met by protests and not to be let into the school by the National Guard?

7. What is the name of the 1954 law which established that racial segregation in schools was unconstitutional?
a. Smith v Board of Education   b. Johnson v Board of Education
c. Wilson v Board of Education   d. Brown v Board of Education

8. Where did Martin Luther King give his infamous "I have a dream" speech?
a. Bunker Hill Monument, Boston   b. Vietnam Veterans Memorial, Washington
c. Lincoln Memorial, Washington   d. Liberty Bell, Philadelphia

9. In which year was Martin Luther King assassinated?
a. 1966   b. 1968   c. 1970   d. 1972

10. Who assassinated Martin Luther King?
a. Robert Johnson   b. Steven Davis   c. Richard Day Wilson   d. James Earl Ray

11. In which year was the Voting Rights Act for African-Americans signed into law?
a. 1965   b. 1969   c. 1973   d. 1976

12. This black power organisation was founded in Oakland in 1966 by Huey P. Newton and Bobby Seale. The organisation was a revolutionary one that subscribed to an ideology of Black nationalism, socialism, and armed self-defence, especially aimed at police brutality. What was the name of this organisation?

13. What happened at a Woolworth's lunch counter in 1960?

14. What is the name of the first African-American student who enrolled at the University of Mississippi?
a. John Chavis   b. James Meredith   c. Alexander Twilight   d. Jonathan Rogan

15. Who were the "Freedom Riders"?

16. What happened to the bus the Freedom Riders were on when it arrived in Anniston, Alabama?
a. Another bus deliberately drove into it
b. A poison gas grenade was thrown into it
c. A bomb was thrown onto the bus

17. How many days were the "Freedom Riders" sentenced in jail?
a. 30 days   b. 30 weeks   c. 30 months   d. 30 years

18. Which famous civil rights march took place on August 28, 1963?

19. Roughly how many people turned up to this march?
a. 40,000 people   b. 80,000 people   c. 150,000 people   d. 250,000 people

20. Which President signed the Civil Rights Act of 1964 into law?
a. Dwight D. Eisenhower   b. John F. Kennedy
c. Richard Nixon   d. Lyndon B. Johnson

21. What did the Civil Rights Act of 1964 prohibit?

22. The Selma to Montgomery march in 1965 quickly became violent as state troopers attacked the unarmed marchers with billy clubs and tear gas as they went over the county line. What did this day become known as?

23. What did the Civil Rights Act of 1964 change about voting laws?
a. It removed literacy tests as a requirement to vote
b. It removed the minimum income required to vote
c. It removed the requirement for African-American voters to be married

24. What did Malcolm Little, who was influential in the black power movement, become better known as?

25. In which year was this Malcolm assassinated?
a. 1958   b. 1960   c. 1963   d. 1965

26. Thurgood Marshall was the first African-American to do what?
a. Compete in the Olympics   b. Serve on the US Supreme Court
c. Become Chief of Police   d. Run for President

27. The 13th Amendment to the United States made what illegal?

28. What were people called who opposed slavery during the 19th century?
a. Advocates   b. Opponents   c. Revolutionists   d. An abolitionist

29. In which state is the National Civil Rights Museum located?
a. Kentucky   b. North Carolina   c. Tennessee   d. Mississippi

30. What was it called when people had to pay a fee to vote?
a. Voters tax   b. Poll tax   c. Balloting tax   d. Choosing tax

31. What does NAACP stand for?

32. What was the name of the leader, born in 1856, who helped to form schools to educate African-Americans in order to improve their status in society?

33. Who was the Civil Rights Act originally proposed by?

34. What was the hotel called where Martin Luther King was assassinated?
a. The Mary Motel   b. The Delilah Motel
c. The Jane Motel   d. The Lorraine Motel

35. What is the name of the campaign, led by Martin Luther King, which was organised in 1963 by the Southern Christian Leadership Conference in an attempt to bring attention to the integration effort of African-Americans in Alabama?
a. Birmingham Campaign   b. Auburn Campaign   c. Mobile Campaign

THE VIETNAM WAR

1. Why did the US become involved with the Vietnam war?

2. What was the name of the leader of South Vietnam until 1963?
a. Nguyen Khanh   b. Duong Van Minh   c. Bao Dai   d. Ngo Dinh Diem

3. What was the name of the leader of north Vietnam until 1963?

4. What is the name of the program whose aim was to prevent Vietcong from using southern villagers to help them hide in the countryside, causing villagers to be removed from their villages and placed into strategic hamlets?
a. Strategic Othello Program   b. Strategic Hamlet Program
c. Strategic MacBeth Program   d. Strategic Coriolanus Program

5. The Tet Offensive was one of the largest military campaigns of the Vietnam War. In which year did it start?
a. 1968   b. 1970   c. 1972   d. 1974

6. Which two countries provided supplies and weapons to the Vietcong?

7. Which deadly chemical herbicide did the US use, which still affects many of the offspring of those originally who were originally exposed today?
a. Agent Red   b. Agent Yellow   c. Agent Orange   d. Agent Black

8. Which country occupied Vietnam before the start of the Vietnam War?

9. What is the name of the type of warfare, where small groups of combatants use different military tactics such as sabotage and ambush to fight a larger and less-mobile military unit, which was regularly used by the Northern Vietnamese?

10. What is the name of the assistance program, implemented by U.S. Pres. Dwight D. Eisenhower in 1954, which had the aim to aid South Vietnam through psychological warfare and paramilitary activities?

11. In which year did North and South Vietnam become the Socialist Republic of Vietnam?
a. 1972   b. 1974   c. 1976   d. 1978

12. What is the name of the massacre where US soldiers killed approximately 500 unarmed villagers in the hamlet of My Lai, Quang Ngai?

13. What was the name of the Chinese communist leader who supported North Vietnam?

14. Which year did the Vietnam war end?
a. 1974   b. 1975   c. 1976   d. 1977

15. Men between which ages were vulnerable of being drafted to the Vietnam War?
a. 18 - 26 years old   b. 18 - 30 years old
c. 16 - 25 years old   d. 17 - 28 years old

THE SPACE RACE

1. In which year did the Space Race officially begin?
a. 1951   b. 1953   c. 1955   d. 1956

2. Which countries competed in the Space Race?

3. Who was the first American to orbit the Earth in 1962?
a. James Reynolds   b. Sam Fitzpatrick   c. Will Dean   d. John Glenn

4. What is the name of the first person to journey to outer space?
a. Virgil Grissom   b. Yuri Gagarin   c. Gherman Titov   d. Andriyan Nikolayev

5. When was the first satellite launched into space?
a. 1957   b. 1958   c. 1959   d. 1960

6. What was the name of this satellite?
a. Vanguard II   b. Titos I   c. Voyager II   d. Sputnik I

7. In 1965, the first person left their space capsule and floated freely in orbit. Which country did he come from?

8. Which American President set the goal of putting a man on the moon by the end of the 1960s?

9. Which of the following was the name of the first American satellite launched in 1958?
a. Gemini I   b. Wanderer I   c. Jupiter I   d. Explorer I

10. What does NASA stand for?

11. Who was the first person to walk on the moon?

12. A dog was one of the first animals to make it to space. What was the name of this dog?

13. Millions of households bought televisions to watch the moon landing. Just how many people tuned in to see man's first step on the moon?
a. 500 million   b. 650 million   c. 800 million   d. 950 million

14. Which President rang the first men to walk on the moon, just minutes after landing?

15. As the International Space Station orbits Earth, how does it generate electricity?

16. In which year was NASA founded?
a. 1956   b. 1957   c. 1958   d. 1959

17. Which of the following is the name of the ship which first took man to space, orbiting the earth?
a. Kranov I   b. Barclav I   c. Vristi I   d. Vostok I

18. Which country sent the first women into space?
a. U.S.   b. USSR   c. France   d. Ukraine

19. How long did it take Apollo 11 to get to the moon?
a. 1 day   b. 3 days   c. 5 days   d. 7 days

20. What is the name of the non-existent line which separates the Earth's atmosphere from outer space?

HISTORY OF SCIENCE

1. What is the name of the person who discovered the X-ray?

2. In which year did Einstein discover the theory of relativity?
a. 1905   b. 1910   c. 1915   d. 1920

3. What is Isaac Newton well known for discovering after being hit on the head by an apple?

4. In which year did Steve Jobs and Steve Wozniak start Apple Computers, Inc?
a. 1976   b. 1979   c. 1982   d. 1985

5. French engineer Georges Claude invented which type of light in 1910?

6. The Greek philosopher Democritus introduced the idea of the atom. In which year was this?
a. 740 BC   b. 400 BC   c. 80 BC   d. 210 AD

7. What species of bird did Charles Darwin famously study?
a. Finches   b. Crows   c. Doves   d. Pigeons

8. Who created the first successful vaccine for polio?

9. What is Stephen Hawking most well-known for?

10. What is the name of Charles Darwin's theory which is a branching pattern of evolution, where individuals with more desirable characteristics to their surroundings survive and breed, causing the species to adapt and evolve over many generations?

11. Hans Lippershey is generally thought to be the inventor of the telescope. In which century did he make this breakthrough?
a. 14th   b. 15th   c. 16th   d. 17th

12. Who is credited with discovering penicillin?

13. How did this man accidentally discover penicillin?

14. Both Alexander Graham Bell and Elisha Gray submitted patent applications regarding which essential piece of technology in 1876?

15. This person, born in 1706, was a famous scientist and inventor among many other things. He was a pioneer in the field of electricity, inventing the lightning rod in 1753. He is also credited with inventing the first stove, as well as greatly innovating bifocals. What was his name?

16. Luc Montagnier was awarded the Noble Prize in 2008 for his work researching which virus?
a. Ebola   b. HIV   c. SARS   d. Zika

17. What is the name of the Ancient Greek mathematician who discovered that, in a right-angled triangle, the square of the hypotenuse is equal to the sum of the square of the other two shorter sides?

18. The smallpox vaccine was the world's first successful vaccine. In which year was the vaccine for smallpox created?
a. 1752   b. 1768   c. 1782   d. 1796

19. What is the name of the person who invented the smallpox vaccine?

20. Marie Curie is remembered for her contribution to finding cancer treatments. Which two elements was she also known for discovering?
a. Uranium   b. Radium   c. Polonium   d. Radon   d. Boron

21. Nicolaus Copernicus put forward which theory about the sun?

22. What is the name of the two people who discovered the structure of DNA in 1953?

23. In 1996 the first animal was cloned. What was the name of the sheep?

24. In which century did the Dutch optician, Hans Jansen, and his son invent the first compound microscope?
a. 15th century   b. 16th century   c. 17th century   d. 18th century

25. Which of the following people is considered by many to be the world's first scientist?
a. Plato   b. Aristotle   c. Darius   d. Archimedes

HISTORY OF MEDICINE

1. Who is considered to be the father of modern medicine?
a. Galen   b. Paracelsus   c. Avicenna   d. Hippocrates

2. Up until the 18th century doctors followed medical theory from Ancient Greece including the theory of the four humours. Phlegm, yellow bile, and black bile made up three of the four humours (liquids). What is the fourth humour called?

3. Name the person who first discovered the bacterium responsible for tuberculosis.
a. Karl Müller   b. Ernst Ehrenbaum   c. Justus von Liebig   d. Robert Koch

4. What did the surgical technique of Trepanning (or trephination) involve?
a. Removing up to a litre of 'bad blood' from the body
b. Removal of an appendix after multiple stomach aches
c. Creating a small hole in the skull

5. What is the name of the person who famously discovered a water pump as the source of a cholera outbreak in 1854?

6. Which year was the X-ray first discovered?
a. 1875   b. 1885   c. 1895   d. 1905

7. Which organ was the first to be successfully transplanted in 1954?
a. Heart   b. Appendix   c. Liver   d. Kidney

8. Louise Brown of Oldham England was the world's first test tube baby. In which year was she born?
a. 1978   b. 1982   c. 1985   d. 1988

9. Who first identified DNA and called it "nuclein"?

10. In which year did Leonard Thompson, a 14-year-old boy dying from type 1 diabetes, receive the first injection of insulin?
a. 1922   b. 1932   c. 1942   d. 1952

11. What was the name of the first female doctor to graduate in the UK?
a. Sarah Findley   b. Gertrude Pieterson   c. Garrett Anderson

12. Åke Senning implanted the first successful pacemaker into a 40-year-old patient. In which year did this occur?
a. 1928   b. 1938   c. 1948   d. 1958

13. This British surgeon was born in 1827. He was not an exceptional surgeon, but he was a pioneer in preventing infection and was the first to practice the science of germ theory during surgery. His antisepsis system is the basis of modern infection management. What is his name?

14. Dr Joseph Murray performed the first successful human transplant of which organ on identical twins in 1954?
a. Liver   b. Kidney   c. Pancreas   d. Adrenal glands

15. Although there have been countless attempts at anaesthesia for surgery, dating back as far as 4000 BC, William T. G. Morton made history in 1846 when he became the first person to successfully perform anaesthesia to perform his surgery. Which liquid did he use as his anaesthetic?

16. Although the x-ray was discovered many years before, it took a while for the ultrasound to be used for medical diagnosis. In which year was the first diagnosis made using an ultrasound?
a. 1936   b. 1946   c. 1956   d. 1966

17. When were leeches first used in medicine?
a. 2500 BC   b. 1500 BC   c. 500 BC   d. 500 AD

18. In which year was the first MRI scan performed on a human?
a. 1977   b. 1984   c. 1990   d. 1997

19. In which year was smallpox eradicated?
a. 1960   b. 1970   c. 1980   d. 1990

20. Dr Christiaan Barnard performed the first human heart transplant when he implanted the heart of a fatally injured 25-year-old woman into 52-year-old South African Lewis Washkansky. In which year did this take place?
a. 1958   b. 1961   c. 1964   d. 1967

21. Which class A drug was often used to cure hay fever in the 19th century?

22. In 2006 the first vaccine to target a cause of cancer was created. What type of cancer was this for?
a. Cervical cancer   b. Breast cancer   c. Lung cancer   d. Testicular cancer

23. Who wrote the first known anatomy book in around the year 300 BC, which is titled Anatomica?

24. Salvino D'Armate is said to have invented the first glasses which were made with a glass-like crystal stone and had a handle to hold up to your eye. In which century did he make this breakthrough?
a. 12th   b. 13th   c. 14th   d. 15th

25. In which year was the rabies vaccine first used to treat a patient?
a. 1872   b. 1885   c. 1897   d. 1909

HISTORY OF THE ARTS

1. Which art movement was Salvador Dali part of?
a. Dadaism   b. Impressionism   c. Harlem Renaissance   d. Surrealism

2. Which Italian renaissance painter pained The Birth of Venus in 1485?

3. What is the name of the artist who painted "The Last Supper"?

4. Andy Warhol was a popular artist during the 1950s, what type of art did he famously create?
a. Rococo   b. Pop Art   c. Installation Art   d. Neon Art

5. Who painted Starry Night in 1889?

6. Edward Munch and Vincent Van Gogh were artists from which art period?
a. Expressionism   b. Futurism   c. Baroque   d. Precisionism

7. This Dutch painter was born in 1606. He is best known for his painting The Night Watch which can be found in Rijksmuseum in Amsterdam. What is his name?

8. Which artist from the neo-impressionist movement painted "A Sunday Afternoon on the Island of La Grande Jatte"?
a. Paul Cézanne   b. Edgar Degas   c. Édouard Manet   d. Georges Seurat

9. Who is known as the "Renaissance man"?

10. This Mexican painter was best known for her portraits and self-portraits. Born in 1907, she explored questions of postcolonialism, identity, gender, race and class in Mexican society. What is her name?

11. Where did Rococo art come from?
a. America   b. Germany   c. Japan   d. France

12. In which century did Dutch Baroque painter Johannes Vermeer live?
a. 16th century   b. 17th century   c. 18th century   d. 19th century

13. In which year did the Romanticism period start?
a. 1770   b. 1820   c. 1840   d. 1860

14. What is the name of the Romantic poet who wrote poems such as The Lamb in 1789 and The Sick Rose in 1794?

15. Which art movement is considered to be the beginning of modern art?
a. Classicism   b. Futurism   c. Impressionism   d. Surrealism

16. What is Realism art?

17. "The Stone Breaker" is an example of Realism art. What is the name of the artist who painted this piece?
a. Henri Matisse   b. Henri Rousseau   c. Georges Seurat   d. Gustave Courbet

18. In which year did Da Vinci paint The Last Supper?
a. 1328   b. 1384   c. 1435   d. 1497

19. This French painter painted Impression, Sunrise in 1872 and La Grenouillère in 1869. What is his name?

20. Henri Matisse was an example of an artist from what movement?
a. Fauvism   b. Classicism   c. Baroque   d. Avant-garde

21. In which year was the Mona Lisa painting stolen from the Louvre in Paris?
a. 1905   b. 1911   c. 1917   d. 1920

22. This Spanish painter painted classics such as La Vie in 1903 and Ma Jolie in 1912. What was his name?

23. "The Kiss" was created by which famous art Nouveau artist?

24. The world's highest price for a piece of artwork - Jackson Pollock's No. 5, 1948 - sold for how much?
a. $140 million   b. $12 million   c. $86 million   d. $6 million

25. James Abbott McNeill Whistler painted his mother Anna McNeill Whistler to make the world-famous painting Whistler's Mother. In which year did he paint this?
a. 1694   b. 1762   c. 1828   d. 1871

26. Who painted the Girl with a Pearl Earring in 1665?

27. How many versions of Edvard Munch's "The Scream" are there?
a. 2   b. 4   c. 6   d. 8

28. Who is considered to be the most famous graffiti artist, whose real identity is still not known?

29. During a mental breakdown in 1888, which body part did Van Gogh cut off?
a. Nose   b. Finger   c. Toe   d. Ear

30. The oldest examples of figurative art can be found in Indonesia which were painted with ochre 45,000 years ago. Which animals did they paint?
a. Cows   b. Pigs   c. Elephants   d. Crocodiles

FAMOUS EXPLORERS

1. Ferdinand Magellan was a Portuguese explorer who is credited as being the first to do what?
a. Travel the whole world   b. Have a child in every continent
c. Travel across the Atlantic   d. Kill a polar bear

2. What is the main role of a cartographer?

3. In what year did Captain Cook first start exploring?
a. 1758   b. 1768   c. 1778   d. 1788

4. What was the main objective of Captain Cook's first journey?
a. To expand the British Empire   b. To observe the planet Venus
c. To live onboard a ship for a year   d. To discover new crops

5. What was the name of the Spanish and Portuguese explorer-soldiers during the 15th and 16th centuries?

6. How did Captain Cook die?
a. From scurvy   b. Suicide   c. A blood infection   d. An attack by a mob

7. Roald Amundsen was the first explorer to reach where?

8. In 1953, the first explorers reached the summit of Mount Everest. What was the name of these two explorers?

9. What is the name of the Italian explorer who accidentally discovered a route from Europe to the Americas?

10. Who was the first woman to fly over the Atlantic Ocean?

11. The Phoenicians were one of the earliest civilisations to start exploring. In what year did they start to explore?
a. 1400 BCE   b. 1500 BCE   c. 1600 BCE   d. 1700 BCE

12. What was the name of the female explorer that left Britain to explore West Africa to find new animal species in the 19th century?

13. Gertrude Bell was an English explorer in the 19th century. Which region did she famously explore to learn more about the people and the history of the region?

14. Jacques-Yves Cousteau is the most famous explorer in which region?
a. Space   b. Antarctica   c. The oceans   d. The Himalayas

15. How many new species of plants and animals were found in the Lewis and Clark Expedition?

16. Who was the first explorer to sail in the Antarctic region?

17. Explorer Vasco de Gama became the first European explorer to reach which country?
a. China   b. Morocco   c. Mexico   d. India

18. The Terra Nova, a whaler and polar expedition ship, is best known for carrying what expedition?

19. Scottish explorer Mungo Park was the first Westerner to have travelled to the central portion of which African river?
a. Niger   b. Congo   c. Nile   d. Zambezi

20. Florida was discovered in 1513 by the first Governor of which territory?

HISTORY OF RELIGION

1. What are the oldest known religious texts in the world?
a. The Bible   b. The Quran   c. The Pyramid Texts   d. The Ancient Scripture

2. What was the earliest Indian religion?
a. Hinduism   b. Sanskrit   c. Vedic   d. Buddhism

3. The Dead Sea Scrolls were discovered at the Qumran Caves in the mid 1900's. They were ancient manuscripts for which religion?

4. How are broad changes in religious and philosophical thought often referred to?
a. The Axial Age   b. The Renaissance   c. The Kuhn Phase   d. The Tudor Shift

5. During which Empire did Christianisation begin to take place?

6. Siddartha Gautama was the founder of which religion?

7. What is the largest religion in the world?

8. Where do historians believe Islam originated?

9. Which religion is believed to be the oldest?

10. Hinduism and Buddhism originate from which country?

11. What European city first experienced Christian preaching?
a. Bethlehem   b. Jerusalem   c. Philippi   d. Ankara

12. Saint Thomas is believed to have introduced what religion to India?

13. What religion has the sacred book of the Torah?

14. What religious event is believed to have happened on Mount Sinai?
a. The murder of Abel
b. God gave Moses the Ten Commandments
c. Noah shepherding the animals onto the Ark
d. The Prophet Muhammad being visited by the angel Jibreel

15. 'Positivism', the Religion of Humanity, was founded by which French philosopher?

16. Theodor Herzl started which religious movement with the aim to establish a Jewish State in Palestine?

17. In which year did Islam start?
a. 610   b. 620   c. 640   d. 660

18. Who was the founder of Judaism?

19. What religion did Sikhism rise out of?

20. How many human gurus are in Sikhism?
a. 4   b. 8   c. 10   d. 13

21. Rastafari is the smallest religion, on average how many followers does it have?
a. 600   b. 6000   c. 60,000   d. 600,000

22. Ashoka the Great spread Buddhism outside of India, how did he do this?

23. What three religions make up the Abrahamic Religions?

24. In what year was Catholicism founded?
a. 20 AD   b. 30 AD   c. 40 AD   d. 50 AD

25. Who is the founder of Confucianism?

HISTORY OF PLAGUES

1. Name the pandemic which killed about half the world's population in the 6th century.

2. How many people did this plague kill?
a. 6 million   b. 25 million   c. 48 million   d. 11 million

3. In what year did the Black Death begin?
a. 1347   b. 1357   c. 1367   d. 1377

4. What infection is believed to have caused the Black Death plague?

5. How was the Black Death passed to humans?

6. How many people did the Black Plague kill?
a. 30 million   b. 40 million   c. 50 million   d. 60 million

7. In 1629, troops from the Thirty Years' War carried the plague into what Italian city?
a. Mantua   b. Florence   c. Naples   d. Rome

8. The Italian Plague began in 1629, what year did it end?
a. 1631   b. 1635   c. 1637   d. 1640

9. What was the Italian Plague also known as? The Great Plague of...
a. Death   b. Milan   c. Hell   d. Boils

10. Which city in Italy experienced particularly high deaths during the Italian Plague?

11. Homes were marked with a red cross during the Gret Plague of London. What did the cross mean?

12. How did The Great Plague of Marseille arrive?
a. With the circus   b. From a ship   c. From rotten fruit   d. From rats

13. The Third Plague Pandemic started in China in which year?
a. 1701 b. 1923 c. 1855 d. 1652

14. Alexandre Yersin identified the cause of the Black Death in which location in 1885?
a. Norway b. Canada c. Austria d. Hong Kong

15. How many worldwide deaths did The Third Plague Pandemic have?
a. 10 million b. 13 million c. 15 million d. 20 million

 # GENERAL KNOWLEDGE

1. What was the largest empire in history?
a. The Ottoman b. The British c. The Absynnian d. The Mongol

2. Which Revolution started in 1789?

3. In which year did the Mexican Revolution begin?
a. 1905 b. 1910 c. 1915 d. 1920

4. What was the name of the Ukrainian power plant that experienced a nuclear disaster in 1986?

5. Which year did the Titanic sink?
a. 1912 b. 1918 c. 1922 d. 1925

6. Athens and Sparta fought in which war?
a. The Peloponnesian War b. Battle of Troy c. The Persian Wars

7. What was Martin Luther King Jr's birth name?
a. Martin b. Michael c. Matthew d. Micah

8. In what country did the first Industrial Revolution take place?

9. What did Philo Farnsworth invent in 1927?
a. The radio b. The microwave c. The television d. The car

10. In 1963, US President John F. Kennedy was assassinated. Which city was he assassinated in?

11. When the Hollywood sign was built in 1923, what did it originally say?
a. Land of the Free   b. Hollywoodland   c. The Hills   d. The Wood

12. Which city held the first modern-day Summer Olympic Games?

13. Why is Mahatma Gandhi famous?

14. Who served as the first President of South Africa?

15. The Anglo-Zanzibar War was a conflict between the United Kingdom and the Zanzibar Sultanate in 1896. How long did this war last?
a. Between 38 and 45 seconds   b. Between 38 and 45 minutes
c. Between 38 and 45 hours   c. Between 38 and 45 days

16. What was the name of the ship that Charles Darwin set sail on in 1831?
a. HMS Beagle   b. HMS Darwin   c. HMS Canary   d. HMS Sparrow

17. Greenland was colonised by what country until 1981?

18. How many days of the week did the ancient Romans have?
a. 4   b. 6   c. 8   d. 10

19. Which US President was president for 32 days?
a. Martin Van Buren   b. Millard Fillmore
c. William Harrison   d. Chester Arthur

20. What is the name of the first bridge to be built along the River Thames?

21. Four US presidents have been assassinated. Can you name them all?

22. Who ruled China the longest?
a. The Shang Dynasty   b. The Zhou Dynasty   c. The Han Dynasty   d. Mao

23. In which year did The Easter Rising in Ireland take place?
a. 1916   b. 1920   c. 1923   d. 1926

24. On 14 July 1789, a state prison on the east side of Paris was stormed. What is the name of the infamous prison?

25. What was Tasmania's original name?

26. Approximately how many passengers died on the Titanic?
a. 500   b. 1000   c. 1500   d. 2000

27. What is the name of the oldest civilization in the world?

28. What did Joan of Arc say before she was burnt at the stake?
a. 'For freedom!'   b. 'For France!'   c. 'Jesus!'   d. 'I regret nothing'

29. What was Bangladesh called before independence?

30. Where was the largest T-Rex skeleton found?

31. How long was the longest war in history?
a. 78 years   b. 112 years   c. 309 years   d. 781 years

32. The Khmer Rouge was a regime that ruled Cambodia in the 20th century. What was the name of the Marxist dictator who lead the brutal regime?

33. Attila the Hun, the 5th century AD conqueror, was known as what?

34. Marco Polo was the first Western explorer to reach what country?

35. Which human ancestor discovered fire?
a. Homo neanderthalensis   b. Homo habilis
c. Homo sapien   d. Homo erectus

36. What happened in the Space Shuttle Challenger disaster?

37. What was the only country in Africa to withstand European colonialism?

38. Che Guevara was an Argentinian with a notable role in which Revolution?

39. England sent convicts to which country between 1788 and 1868?
a. Ireland   b. Australia   c. India   d. Jamaica

40. What was Mumbai previously known as?

41. Which country did Argentina fight against in the Falklands War?

42. What did George Stephenson invent in 1814?
a. Steam Engine   b. Light bulb   c. Telephone   d. Phonograph

43. In 1913 a woman threw herself in front of the King's horse at Epsom Derby to protest against women's suffrage. What is the name of this woman?

44. How many people have been trained as astronauts as of 2022?
a. 200   b. 400   c. 600   d. 800

45. In 1930, the first FIFA World Cup took place. Which country won?
a. Brazil   b. Uruguay   c. Argentina   d. Portugal

46. What is the name of the rebellion which involved gold miners revolting against the British administration of the colony of Victoria, Australia?

47. Which European country was the first to legalise same-sex marriage?

48. What was the first pyramid the Egyptians ever built?

49. Who was the first prime minister of India?

50. What was Ho Chi Minh city previously known as?

51. Which year did Frida Kahlo die?
a. 1944   b. 1954   c. 1964   d. 1974

52. In the 1936 Olympics, Jessie Owens won four gold medals. Who did this infuriate?

ANSWERS

PRE-HISTORY

1. The Stone Age came first (around 2.5 million years ago), followed by the Bronze Age (around 4000 years ago), followed by the Iron Age (3000 around years ago).

2. b - 10 million years ago

3. False - Humans were around 65 million years after the dinosaurs were extinct.

4. d - At least 5

5. d - Cretaceous

6. Pre-history ended when humans settled into agricultural societies and began to write.

7. b - Flute

8. a - Homo floresiensis

9. b - Homo Erectus

10. c - Ancient Greek

ANCIENT EGYPT

1. The Rosetta Stone
2. Alexander the Great
3. The Book of the Dead
4. Howard Carter
5. a - The River Nile provided a fertile floodplain which created productive farmland for the civilisations
6. b - 1922
7. c - Scribes and officials
8. c - 20th Dynasty
9. d - Her name was Sekhmet and was the goddess of destruction
10. a - 0 were found, they had all been stolen years before
11. c - Anubis
12. a - The brain
13. Salt
14. c - Sand and linin
15. a - It symbolised protection from evil
16. Shemu which is the harvest season
17. a - 2649–2130 B.C
18. The Valley of the Kings
19. b - Cobra
20. c - Akhenaten
21. d - Malaria
22. a & d - Julius Caesar and Mark Antony
23. c - 30 BC
24. A snake
25. b - 19
26. c - His tomb was undisturbed for 3000 years
27. c - 10 years
28. a - The Karnak Temple Complex

29. b - They believed writing was a gift from Thoth, the ibis-headed god of wisdom

30. Pictures were often used as most of the Egyptian population could not read

31. b - Memphis

32. b - The word hieroglyphic comes from Ancient Greek and means sacred symbol

33. d - The Egyptians worshipped more than 2000 gods and goddesses

34. All the mummies had been stolen by graverobbers

35. c - Polytheism

36. c - The Great Pyramid was finished around 2566 BCE

37. c - Hatshepsut

38. b - Lion

39. Honey

40. c - 2, but they were both stillborn

41. It is a curse alleged to curse anyone who disturbs the mummy of an ancient Egyptian. It is claimed to cause illness, bad luck, or death

42. b - 6650 km

43. They believed the soul was judged for its goodness by the God Anubis. Anubis would weigh the heart of the dead person to measure how good they had been in life

44. d - The Hittites

45. A dung beetle

46. c - Jean-François Champollion

47. Akhenaten

48. The slaves pulled the heavy materials across the dessert by creating a sledge

49. b - The Pyramid of Djoser (The Step Pyramid of Djoser)

50. True

ANCIENT GREECE

1. Sparta was the enemy of Athens
2. d - 1896
3. King Darius I
4. a - Pella, Macedonia
5. d - Socrates died from poisoning after drinking hemlock
6. Sparta
7. c - Hephaestus
8. b - Pericles
9. a - The sacrifice of 100 oxen to the God Zeus would take place
10. Alexander the Great conquered the city of Tyre.
11. c - Cronus
12. Mount Olympus
13. b - An olive wreath
14. d - Omega
15. Athena
16. c - 12 Gods and Goddesses
17. Greeks called themselves Hellenes- it was the Romans that called them Greeks
18. It is believed the Greeks invented the yo-yo
19. The Parthenon
20. True
21. A three-headed dog that guarded the gates to the underworld
22. a - The boys were 7 years old when they began their training
23. Socrates
24. The war was between the early Greeks and the People of Troy
25. Zeus
26. Homer
27. The Delian League
28. b - 323 BC
29. Togas
30. The Greek alphabet derived from the North Semitic alphabet via that of the Phoenicians

31. Fall in love
32. a - Demeter
33. True
34. a - Beauty and love
35. c - Lion
36. c - Iasonas
37. c - Uranus
38. a - Sophocles
39. Aristotle
40. b - The birthplace of democracy
41. Acropolis
42. b - Euclid
43. Hippocrates
44. b - Triremes
45. a - A military formation
46. d - They believed they contained the souls of the dead
47. a & d - Doric and Ionic
48. a - Pheidippides
49. Handshakes
50. a - Epeius

CELTIC BRITAIN

1. Celtic tribes signed a peace treaty with Alexander the Great, ensuring peace between the Celts and the Greeks
2. d - Brythonic (also called Britons), who lived around modern-day Cornwall and Wales
3. Welsh
4. c - The Iron Age
5. c - Druidism
6. a - A druid was a member of the high-ranking class in ancient Celtic cultures
7. c - 43 AD
8. b - Barbarians
9. d - Danu
10. c - Early sources place the Celts in Western and Central Europe, then expanding to live across most of Europe during the Iron Age. Over several years they spread outwards, taking over France and Belgium, and coming over to Britain
11. a - The Romans
12. d - Over 300 Gods
13. a - The Celtic Triskele is a common motif in Celtic art and traditions. It is a triple spiral that has rotational symmetry
14. b - Queen Boudica
15. b - Iceni

THE ROMANS

1. a - 753 BC
2. Augustus
3. Latin
4. Emperor Diocletian
5. d - Jupiter
6. d - Emperor Constantine
7. c - 7 hills
8. b - 15th
9. Romulus and his twin brother Remus
10. Flavian Amphitheater
11. Pluto
12. d - 80 AD
13. The Appian Way
14. a - Chariot races and gladiatorial displays
15. b - Gladius
16. c - Crassus
17. d - Nero
18. Caligula
19. a - Constantine I (Rome's first Christian Emperor)
20. a - Denarius
21. Cohort
22. b - Mars
23. c - Virgil
24. c - Calpurnia
25. a - Ermin Way
26. b - Senators
27. c - 23 times
28. d - Frumentarii
29. b - Venus
30. a & e - Hadrian and Antonine
31. Pompeii
32. Carthage and Rome
33. a - Coin
34. Pax Romana
35. b - Minerva
36. b - Little boot
37. To protect the Emperor and his family
38. d - Vespasian
39. Neptune
40. c - Law of the Twelve Tables
41. Magnentius
42. b - Nero
43. a - Hagia Sophia
44. a - 4
45. c - Patricians
46. d - The Forum
47. Jesus
48. c - The Meditations
49. a - 44 BCE
50. Third Servile War

THE ANGLO-SAXONS

1. b - The Normans
2. a - 410-1066 AD
3. Harold Godwinson
4. Battle of Hastings
5. d - Germany
6. b - Old English
7. Beowulf
8. c - Alfred the Great
9. a,d & f - Angles, Saxons, and Jutes
10. William the Conqueror
11. The early Anglo-Saxons were pagans but they converted to Christianity in 595AD
12. c - Runic Script
13. d - 1042 AD
14. Wessex
15. Cyning

THE VIKINGS

1. b - Scandinavia
2. d - 793 - 1066
3. b - Drakkar
4. Leif Erikson
5. a - Odin
6. A hammer
7. a - Around the 11th century
8. c - Longships
9. The Viking heaven
10. Erik the Red
11. d - A raven
12. b - 874 AD
13. a - 3 classes, these were called thrall, karl, and jarl
14. c - Old Norse
15. Harald Bluetooth

THE MONGOL EMPIRE

1. Genghis Khan
2. d - 9 million square miles
3. b - 16 million
4. b - Karakorum
5. b & d - Tengrism and Buddhism
6. b - 1227
7. a - 1368
8. True
9. d - Bow and arrow
10. They were called Khanates, and the four were: Golden Hordes in the Northeast, Yuan Dynasty or Great Khanate in China, Ilkhanate in the Southeast and Persia, and the Chagatai Khanate in Central Asia.

THE OTTOMAN EMPIRE

1. a - 1299
2. d - 36
3. c - Istanbul
4. b - Osman I
5. d - Islam
6. c - Mehmed II
7. b - The Ottoman Empire was founded in Anatolia, now modern-day Turkey
8. The Ottoman Empire ended after its defeat in World War I
9. After the peak of Ottoman rule in the 16th century, the empire struggled to maintain its bureaucracy and political structure
10. a - 1922

THE AZTECS

1. c - The Aztecs would sacrifice still-beating hearts from sacrificial victims
2. b - Mexico
3. The Tenochca or the Mexica
4. a - Nahuatl language
5. d - 1428
6. b - 1521
7. a - Huitzilopochtli
8. d - Cuauhtémoc also known as Cuauhtemotzín, Guatimozín, or Guatémoc
9. Spanish
10. b - Smallpox
11. d - Maize
12. c - God of rain and fertility
13. c - Tenochtitlan
14. d - Agriculture and trading
15. d - To please the gods

THE RENAISSANCE

1. a - Florence, Italy
2. The Medici family
3. Leonardo da Vinci
4. c - Renaissance is the French word for rebirth
5. a - 14th century
6. a - Francesco Petrarca
7. d - Humanism was the main philosophy
8. b - The height of the Renaissance was called the "High Renaissance", as this was the time when the most notable artworks were produced
9. d - Michelangelo
10. Protestantism
11. c - 17th century
12. The printing press
13. b - Niccolò Machiavelli
14. Galileo Galilei
15. The Mona Lisa
16. Michel de Montaigne
17. The Black Death or bubonic plague
18. William Shakespeare
19. Christopher Columbus
20. d - Sculptures

THE INCA EMPIRE

1. Machu Picchu
2. b - 15th-century
3. South America - more specifically the Peruvian highlands
4. c - 12 million inhabitants
5. d - 1572
6. d - The rain God
7. d - Cuzco, also spellt Cusco and Kosko
8. a - Manco Capac
9. d - Llama and alpaca wool
10. c - Quechua
11. a - Viracocha
12. False - each individual state had its own government which had its own state laws.
13. b - 25,000 miles
14. Quipu was a system that used knotted string to signify a certain amount of information. Exactly what information it was recording is unknown
15. d - 1438

THE TUDORS

1. d - Richard III
2. Anne Boleyn and Catherine Howard
3. a - Edward VI was 9 years old when he became king
4. c - The Globe Theatre
5. Bloody Mary- this was down to her persecution of Protestants
6. c - 1587
7. b - Pembroke Castle
8. d - House of Lancaster
9. The Virgin Queen
10. b - 9 days

11. d - Thomas Cromwell
12. a - Thomas Cranmer was burnt at the stake for heresy
13. Anne Boylen
14. Hans Holbein the Younger
15. b - Catherine Parr
16. Utopia
17. b - The Tudor Rose
18. b - The Archbishops
19. c - Henry married 6 times
20. a - Whipping was a common punishment
21. c - 1485
22. b - In total there were six monarchs during the Tudor times
23. b - Henry divorced her because she could not give Henry a son
24. c - Six months
25. c - Henry banned ordinary people from playing sports. They were only allowed to play sports at Christmas time
26. Blackened teeth became fashionable during the Tudor times because they believed they showed wealth. Sugar could only be afforded by the wealthiest of people so black teeth showed that they were wealthy
27. c - 35-40 years
28. The Pilgrimage of Grace
29. The Bible
30. Elizabeth I
31. c - Defender of the Faith
32. b - 1549
33. c - 32 years
34. b - The Mary Rose
35. c - Christopher Wren
36. d - A Peacock
37. The Golden Age
38. c - John Cabot
39. a - 1564
40. b - Treason

THE NAPOLEONIC WARS

1. The Battle of Waterloo
2. b - 1769
3. c - The Battle of Borodino
4. Napoleon was exiled to the island of Saint Helena off the coast of Africa
5. b - 51
6. The Duke of Wellington, Arthur Wellesley
7. b - 1814
8. The expression means to be defeated
9. d - 38
10. a - 1804
11. a - The Little Corporal
12. c - The Hundred Days
13. b - Portugal
14. b - 1809
15. d - Stomach cancer

AMERICAN CIVIL WAR

1. a - Around 2% of the population died during the war which is an estimated 620,000 men
2. d - The Battle of Gettysburg
3. The Reconstruction Era
4. Ulysses S. Grant
5. b - Knights of the Golden Circle
6. b - Traveller
7. d - Appomattox Court House
8. a - The Fort Pillow Massacre
9. b - This was the first battle ever between two ironclad warships
10. Gatling gun

11. b - 11 states
12. Texas, Arkansas, Louisiana, Tennessee, Mississippi, Alabama, Georgia, Florida, South Carolina, North Carolina and Virginia
13. b - Union victory
14. d - John Brown's Body
15. c - 1865
16. The Civil War began because of the differences between the free and slave states over the government's power to prohibit slavery in the territories that had not yet become states
17. The Union won the American Civil War
18. b - 10%
19. The Confederate States
20. Jefferson Davis
21. Charleston, South Carolina
22. b - Battle of Harforough Sands
23. a - Mathew Brady
24. a - 620,000
25. b - Virginia
26. John Wilkes Booth
27. b - Lincoln was attending the play "Our American Cousin" at Ford's Theatre
28. Most deaths and casualties were the result of disease. For every three soldiers killed in battle, five more died of disease
29. b - 4 years
30. War Between the States
31. a - The battle took place in 1862
32. c - Battle of Chickamauga
33. True
34. Robert E. Lee
35. a - H.L. Hunley

COLONIALISM

1. French Guiana is still owned by the French
2. b - The 15th century
3. c - Germany
4. d - The British Raj
5. Anglo-Zulu War
6. d - Portugal
7. a - East India Company
8. d - Belize
9. c - Thailand
10. The Netherlands
11. a - 141 million
12. Sri Lanka
13. Bahn mi
14. Kingdom of Eswatini formally Swaziland
15. c - The British Empire ruled more than 458 million people
16. Hawaii
17. c - The 19th century saw the second wave of colonial expansion
18. The Scramble for Africa
19. c - King Leopold II
20. In 1838 the U.S. Government forced the Cherokee west. They were forced to walk thousands of miles and an estimated 4,000 Cherokees died
21. a - The Netherlands
22. Dutch
23. Aboriginals
24. b - 1788
25. c - 3 million
26. b - 1980
27. b - 28,000
28. Britain colonised most countries. The British Empire once covered about one-quarter of all the land on Earth
29. c - The Bahamas gained independence in 1973
30. Kenya

WORLD WAR ONE

1. a - Bulgaria
2. d - 1918
3. Influenza or Spanish flu
4. Triple Entente
5. d - 1917
6. b - She was convicted of spying on Germany's behalf
7. Edith Cavell was an English nurse and became a heroine for improving the standards of nursing
8. Battle of Verdun
9. a - 1915
10. c - The Battle of Passchendaele
11. b - Trenches were dug in zig-zag lines
12. d - The Battle of the Somme
13. H. H. Asquith
14. c - Frank Woodruff Buckles
15. Russia
16. c - 1917
17. Italy
18. d - The United States did not join the organisation
19. Wilhelm II
20. b - Poison gas
21. Germany, Austria-Hungary, and Italy
22. Treaty of Versailles
23. a - Mustard Gas
24. Woodrow Wilson
25. Dogfights were aerial battles between fighter aircraft
26. Armistice Day was Friday, November 11, 1918
27. d - Pigeons
28. c - 80
29. Archduke Franz Ferdinand
30. David Lloyd George

WORLD WAR TWO

1. b - 6 million Jewish people were killed
2. d - The Battle of the Atlantic was the longest and lasted 2074 days
3. Auschwitz
4. b - The Soviet Union
5. b - 1939
6. Poland
7. Germany, Italy, and Japan
8. Normandy, France
9. b - Suicide by gunshot
10. b - WW2 lasted for 6 years
11. Alan Turing
12. Victory in Europe Day
13. Britain, France, Russia, China, and the USA
14. c - It was the first battle to be fought entirely by air forces
15. b - Joseph Stalin
16. Dwight D. Eisenhower
17. d - December 07, 1941
18. Joseph Goebbels
19. c - Approximately 70 million soldiers fought in WW2
20. b - Sweden
21. France
22. The Blitz
23. America
24. a - Hiroshima
25. b - Enola Gay
26. Winston Churchill
27. a - 405,000
28. a - September 02, 1945
29. Yamamoto
30. b - Japan
31. b - 1941
32. a - Treblinka
33. Harry S Truman
34. Poland
35. Russia
36. Marshall Plan
37. b - U-boat
38. Eva Braun
39. d - The Battle of Normandy
40. c - Manhattan Project

THE COLD WAR

1. The United States and the Soviet Union
2. NATO stands for North Atlantic Treaty Organization
3. Limits were set on the number of nuclear missiles and anti-missile systems that could be fired by the U.S. and the Soviet Union
4. Cuba
5. c - Iron Curtain
6. The Western Block was the name of the respective allies of the United States
7. b - The Cold War period began on March 12, 1947
8. d - The Soviet Union formed the Warsaw Pact- a defence treaty formed by the Soviet Union along with seven other Soviet states in Central and Eastern Europe
9. The Berlin Blockade was an attempt by the Soviet Union to limit accessibility to the United States, Great Britain, and France to travel to sectors of the city of Berlin
10. Fidel Castro
11. a - The doctrine was called the Containment Doctrine
12. b - 13 days
13. a - 1949
14. b - 1949
15. d - George Orwell
16. c - The US created the policy of Détente Diplomacy
17. a - 1989
18. b - 1991
19. Mikhail Sergeyevich Gorbachev
20. George H. W. Bush
21. A proxy war is a war started by a major power which itself does not get involved in the war
22. c - The Cold War lasted for 45 years
23. c - The war lasted 9 years
24. b - 1952
25. b - Hungary

THE KOREAN WAR

1. b - 1950
2. a - North Korea was supported by China and the Soviet Union
3. a - Korea was divided into two states- the North and South
4. Communism
5. d - Battle of Ia Drang - this was fought in the Vietnam War
6. a - The United States and allied nations
7. b - 1951
8. c - The line that divides North Korea and South Korea is called 38th parallel
9. b - 3 years
10. The Korean War began when the Northern Korean People's Army invaded South Korea in a coordinated attack along the 38th parallel
11. d - Kim Il-sung was the leader of North Korea
12. d - 38% of American POWs died during the Korean War
13. b - Jet fighters were used in air-to-air combat for the first time in history
14. b - Rhee Syng-man
15. c - Nearly 5 million people died

Civil Rights

1. The Jim Crow laws
2. Rosa Parks
3. Martin Luther King
4. It was a protest in which African-Americans refused to ride city buses to protest segregated seating
5. d - 381 days
6. Little Rock Nine
7. d - Brown v Board of Education
8. c - Lincoln Memorial, Washington
9. b - He was assassinated in 1968
10. d - James Earl Ray assassinated Martin Luther King
11. a - 1965
12. The Black Panthers
13. Four college students refused to leave a Woolworth's lunch counter when they were not served. It became known as the Greensboro sit-ins as hundreds of people joined them
14. b - James Meredith
15. The Freedom Riders were a group of white and African American civil rights activists. They embarked on a bus tour of Southern America to protest segregated bus terminals
16. c - A bomb was thrown onto the bus
17. a - They were sentenced to 30 days in jail
18. The March on Washington
19. d - 250,000 people turned up to the march
20. d - Lyndon B. Johnson
21. Discrimination based on race, colour, sex, nationality and religion
22. Bloody Sunday
23. a - It removed literacy tests as a requirement to vote
24. Malcolm X

25. d - 1965
26. b - Serve on the US Supreme Court
27. Slavery
28. d - An abolitionist
29. c - Tennessee
30. b - Poll tax
31. The National Association for the Advancement of Colored People
32. Booker T. Washington
33. John F. Kennedy
34. d - The Lorraine Motel
35. a - Birmingham Campaign

THE VIETNAM WAR

1. They were worried that communism would spread to South Vietnam and then to the rest of Asia
2. d - Ngo Dinh Diem
3. Ho Chi Minh
4. b - Strategic Hamlet Program
5. a - 1968
6. China and the Soviet Union
7. c - Agent Orange
8. France
9. Guerrilla warfare
10. The Saigon Military Mission
11. c - 1976
12. The Mai Lai Massacre
13. Mao Zedong
14. b - 1975
15. a - 18 - 26 years old

THE SPACE RACE

1. c - 1955
2. The United States and the Soviet Union
3. d - John Glenn
4. b - Yuri Gagarin
5. a - 1957
6. d - Sputnik I
7. Soviet Union
8. John F Kennedy
9. d - Explorer I
10. National Aeronautics and Space Administration
11. Neil Armstrong
12. Laika
13. b - 650 million
14. Richard Nixon
15. The Space station uses solar panels to generate electricity
16. c - 1958
17. d - Vostok I
18. b - USSR
19. b - It took the Apollo 11 astronauts three days, three hours, and 49 minutes to reach the moon
20. Karman Line

HISTORY OF SCIENCE

1. W.C. Röntgen
2. a - 1905
3. Issac Newton is famous for discovering the theory of gravity after an apple fell and hit his head
4. a - 1976
5. Neon lights
6. b - 400 BC
7. a - Finches
8. Jonas Salk
9. Stephen Hawkings is most well-known for working on the physics of black holes
10. Natural selection
11. d - 17th century
12. Alexander Fleming
13. Dr Alexander Fleming found mould growing on a Petri dish of Staphylococcus bacteria. He noticed that the mould seemed to be preventing bacteria from growing around it.
14. The telephone
15. Benjamin Franklin
16. b - Luc Montagnier received a Noble Prize for his research on the HIV virus
17. Pythagoras
18. d - 1796
19. Edward Jenner
20. b & c - radium and polonium
21. Nicolaus Copernicus was the first scientist to propose the earth and other planets revolve around the sun, and that the sun was stationary
22. James Watson and Francis Crick
23. Dolly the sheep
24. b - 16th century
25. b - Aristotle is considered to be the first scientist

HISTORY OF MEDICINE

1. d - Hippocrates
2. Blood
3. d - Robert Koch
4. c - Trepanning involved drilling or scraping a hole into the human skull and was done to either relieve pressure from a build-up of blood or was believed to give a trapped demon a hole to escape
5. John Snow
6. c - The X-ray was discovered in 1895
7. d - The kidney was the first organ to be successfully transplanted
8. a - 1978
9. Johann Friedrich Miescher in 1869
10. a - 1922
11. c - Elizabeth Garrett Anderson
12. d - 1958
13. Joseph Lister
14. b - Kidney
15. Ether
16. c - 1956
17. b - 1500 BC
18. a - 1977
19. c - 1980
20. d - 1967
21. Cocaine
22. a - Cervical cancer
23. Diocles
24. b - 13th century
25. b - 1885

HISTORY OF THE ARTS

1. d - Surrealism
2. Sandro Botticelli
3. Leonardo da Vinci
4. b - Pop art
5. Vincent van Gogh
6. a - Expressionism
7. Rembrandt
8. d - Georges Seurat
9. Leonardo da Vinci
10. Frida Kahlo
11. d - Rococo art originated in Paris, France
12. b - 17th century
13. a - 1770

14. William Blake
15. c - Impressionism
16. Realism attempted to show subjects as they truly existed and in their real light avoiding supernatural and fiction
17. d - Gustave Courbet
18. d - 1497
19. Claude Monet
20. a - The Fauvism movement
21. b - 1911
22. Pablo Picasso
23. Gustav Klimt
24. a - $140 million
25. d - 1871
26. Johannes Vermeer
27. b - There are 4 versions
28. Banksy
29. d - Ear
30. b - Pigs

FAMOUS EXPLORERS

1. a - Travel the whole world
2. Cartographers create and draw up maps. They were vital members of exploration crews
3. b - 1768
4. b - To observe the planet Venus to help astronomers calculate the distance of the Sun from the Earth
5. Conquistador
6. d - An attack by a mob on a Hawaiian island
7. The North Pole
8. New Zealand's Ed Hillary and Darjeeling's Sherpa Tenzing Norgay were the first to reach the summit
9. Christopher Columbus
10. Amelia Earheart
11. b - 1500 BCE
12. Mary Kingsley
13. The Middle East
14. c - The oceans
15. 300
16. William Barents was the first to sail in the Antarctic region
17. d - India
18. The Terra Nova ship is best known for carrying Robert Falcon Scott's 1910 British Antarctic Expedition
19. a - Africa's Niger River
20. Puerto Rico

HISTORY OF RELIGION

1. c - The Pyramid Texts from ancient Egypt date between 2400–2300 BCE
2. c - Vedic
3. The Dead Sea Scrolls are ancient Jewish and Hebrew religious manuscripts.
4. a - The Axial Age
5. It began in the Roman Empire
6. Buddhism
7. Christianity
8. Historians believe Islam originated in Mecca and Medina
9. Hinduism is believed to be the oldest religion founded around the 15th – 5th century BCE
10. India
11. c - Philippi
12. Christianity
13. Judaism
14. b - God gave Moses the Ten Commandments
15. Auguste Comte
16. Zionism
17. a - 610
18. Abraham
19. Hinduism
20. c - 10
21. d - 600,000 followers
22. He sent nine Buddhist expeditions to spread the religion beyond India
23. Christianity, Islam and Judaism
24. b - 30 AD
25. Confucius

HISTORY OF PLAGUES

1. Plague of Justinian
2. b - It is believed to have killed at least 25 million people
3. a - 1347
4. The bacterium Yersinia pestis
5. The Black Death was passed through infected rats that had been bitten by fleas
6. c - 50 million people
7. a - The Italian city of Mantua
8. a - 1631
9. b - The Great Plague of Milan
10. Lombardy
11. The cross meant that the homes were infected and that these people were quarantining
12. b - The disease arrived on a merchant ship called the Grand Saint Antoine
13. c - 1855
14. d - Hong Kong
15. c - 15 million worldwide

GENERAL KNOWLEDGE

1. b - The British Empire
2. The French Revolution
3. b - 1910
4. Chernobyl
5. a - 1912
6. a - The Peloponnesian War
7. b - Michael
8. The United Kingdom
9. c - The television
10. Dallas
11. b - "Hollywoodland" (to promote the name of a new housing development in the hills)
12. Athens
13. Gandhi led his country to freedom from British colonial rule in 1947
14. Nelson Mandela
15. b - Between 38 and 45 minutes
16. a - HMS Beagle
17. Denmark
18. c - 8 days
19. c - William Harrison
20. The London Bridge
21. Abraham Lincoln, James A. Garfield, William McKinley, John F. Kennedy
22. b - The Zhou dynasty (1046- 256 BCE)
23. a - 1916
24. The Bastille
25. Van Diemen's Land
26. c - 1500
27. The Mesopotamia Civilization
28. c - 'Jesus'
29. East Pakistan
30. Canada
31. d - The Reconquista is believed to have gone on for 781 years
32. Pol Pot
33. "The Scourge of God"
34. China
35. d - Homo erectus
36. The shuttle exploded 73 seconds into the flight and killed all 7 members of the crew
37. Ethiopia
38. The Cuban Revolution
39. b - Australia
40. Bombay
41. The United Kingdom
42. a - Steam Engine
43. Emily Davison
44. c - 600 people have been trained as astronauts
45. b - Uraguay
46. The Eureka Stockade
47. The Netherlands
48. The pyramid of Djoser
49. Jawaharlal Nehru
50. Saigon
51. b - 1954
52. Adolf Hitler

Made in the USA
Middletown, DE
24 April 2023